TO TEACH
as Jesus
TAUGHT

John T. Swencki
100 Landham Rd.
Sudbury, MA 01776

TO TEACH *as* *Jesus* TAUGHT

11 ATTRIBUTES OF A MASTER TEACHER

THOMAS A. WAYMENT

CFI
Springville, Utah

Dedication

To Brandi
For sharing the passion to teach

ISBN 13: 978-1-59955-285-9

Published by CFI, an imprint of Cedar Fort, Inc., 2373 W. 700 S., Springville, UT 84663
Distributed by Cedar Fort, Inc. www.cedarfort.com

Library of Congress Cataloging-in-Publication Data

Wayment, Thomas A.
  To teach as Jesus taught : 11 attributes of a master teacher / Thomas A. Wayment.
    p. cm.
  ISBN 978-1-59955-285-9 (acid-free paper)
  1. Teaching--Religious aspects--Christianity. 2. Christian education--Teaching methods. 3. Jesus Christ--Teaching methods. 4. Church of Jesus Christ of Latter-day Saints--Doctrines. I. Title.

  BV1534.W39 2009
  232.9'04--dc22

                                    2009009877

Cover design by Jen Boss
Cover design © 2009 by Lyle Mortimer
Edited by Melissa Caldwell

Printed in the United States of America

10 9 8 7 6 5 4 3 2 1

Printed on acid-free paper

Contents

Introduction

If you knew Jesus as a mortal man, would you have thought of him as a Savior of mankind, as a prophet, as a teacher, or as a crank and charlatan? Although no one can fully answer this question without assuming that one's current beliefs are an indication of how one might have responded, the question reaches to the very heart of what so many people had to ask themselves when they met Jesus for the first time. Among the many questions and answers that may arise from trying to understand Jesus in this way is, "In what capacity was he at his best or what particular talent or attribute defined him most?" Or, in other words, "Where did others perceive his greatest talent to lie as a mortal man and how was he described to others?"

Like those who knew or met him personally in his day, our understanding of him might have hinged on what we perceived to be his particular talent or what we considered to be an obvious weakness. We might have considered him to be a prophet, a leader, or more generally a charismatic and kind person, but today it is sometimes difficult to see through our own understanding—that Jesus is our Lord and Savior—and consider who he was for the many people who knew him in mortality. Maintaining our faith in Jesus Christ is an important part of enduring to the end, but seeing Jesus through the eyes of others, especially through the eyes of those who knew him in the first century, enriches our understanding and sheds new light on a very familiar subject, permitting us to build upon an already sure foundation. If everyone had a single, monolithic understanding of Jesus in his day, then there would likely only be one form of

Christianity. And just like in our day, the decades after Jesus died saw the rise of many different forms of Christianity that more or less remained faithful to their interpretation of Jesus' message.

Although we know him as Savior and God, in Jesus' day there were only a few who thought that he was God or even that he was like God. Many looked at him as simply a talented individual, and some, like Josephus and Tacitus, even wrote testimonies about him as a historic person. They did not see him as the Christ, but rather as an individual who attracted followers and died for his beliefs. Some Roman historians were more interested in why so many would willingly die for such an unknown (and what they considered an unnoteworthy) figure.

Throughout history, Jesus—primarily through the written accounts of his life and his teachings—has been able to touch the lives of billions of individuals, whether rich or poor, famous or infamous, strong or weak. Christians have disagreed about him almost since the moment of his death. The Apostle Paul fought to suppress what he thought were errant forms of Christianity that had grown up in his day and who worshipped, "another Jesus" (2 Corinthians 11:4).

This book will look at Jesus personally, from a new perspective. It is not meant to advocate a predetermined position, although certainly personal biases cannot be suppressed. This book will consider the very question of who Jesus was in the eyes of those who knew him in mortality by examining how they sought to describe him. Some authors thought of him as a new Moses, some accounts focus on his many miracles, and everyone seems to have been captivated by his death.

After reading this volume, I hope you will come away with a greater appreciation of who Jesus was and what impact he had on those who knew him. I also hope that you will see something in his magnificent life that will help you shape something in your own life. In a way, this book looks back at four testimonies and not four autobiographies. Those testimonies—the four Gospels—reveal what Jesus meant to those who loved him and followed him. And one thing that stands out is that his disciples consistently thought of Jesus as a great teacher.

Being a teacher myself, and knowing that everyone who believes in the gospel of Jesus Christ is a teacher, I have found great meaning in thinking about the master teacher. I have improved my own teaching in small ways, and in other ways I am simply more appreciative of what he experienced. I cannot replicate everything that he did, but I am, at least, better informed and less surprised about the personality of the Savior.

A note of consideration is in order at the beginning of this book. From having studied teaching methodology and various approaches, I find it important to mention that the greatest teachers have always considered all aspects of their subjects. The greatest teachers do not consider it a sin to think broadly about their subjects and then to advocate a distinct and clear position concerning a specific viewpoint. Some teachers feel it is their job to simply portray the various attitudes and responses to a certain subject and then to let their students decide what to believe or how to implement it. For those who view teaching in this way, they will be disappointed in the way Jesus taught. He held strong positions and he took a stand on a number of issues. He was frequently, if not always, intimately informed about a variety of subjects. His answers show that he pondered certain subjects from various vantage points, and some answers seem to suggest that he at least considered answers opposite to those he gave.

I hope that you will find greater appreciation for Jesus in reading this book, and that your own approach to advocating his words will be more profound, more ponderous, and more pointed in the spirit of the great Master Teacher.

This book is organized around eleven attributes of Jesus' teaching style. An "at a glance" section is included at the beginning of each chapter and provides details concerning the subject under consideration in a way that will be easily accessible to the reader. Some of those details are implied in the narrative and others will become part of the discussion.

At the end of the book, a short postscript briefly discusses how this particular volume relates to other studies on the life of Jesus. That final chapter will show how far we have come in understanding the full extent of what Jesus has meant to his disciples throughout the centuries and across dispensations.

ATTRIBUTE 1

Understanding Audience

DETAILS OF JESUS' LIFE AT A GLANCE:

- None of Jesus' parables speak of the rich in a positive way.
- The heroes of Jesus' parables are almost always poor.
- Jesus was a "carpenter" (Mark 6:3) meaning he either worked as a stonemason or worked with wood timbers used in houses. Other such artisans in rural Galilee were poor.
- Day laborers—those who hired out each day—figure into Jesus' parables and were the poorest class of citizens above beggars.
- Jesus was declared "Messiah" in Bethany, which literally means the "house of the poor" or the "poorhouse."
- Jesus named only one person in all his parables. The name of that person was Lazarus, the same name of one of Jesus' closest associates. Lazarus was a beggar in the parable.
- Luke informs us that Jesus' ministry was at least partially financed by three generous women donors—Joanna, Susanna, and Mary Magdalene (Luke 8:2–3).

GALILEE: A LAND OF THE OPPRESSED

Immediately, as we look into the story of Jesus we learn that he was champion of the oppressed—an advocate of society's downtrodden and neglected. Popular and powerful teachers have causes, and even though Jesus' primary and ultimate mission was aimed at the salvation of

1

mankind, he frequently directed his messages in mortality to the poor, or he used language that appealed to the poor of his day and age. It is no surprise then that he was loved in the rural regions of Galilee, where life tended to be more harsh and unforgiving, but despised in the metropolis of Jerusalem, where a trade and business economy were well developed. Jesus was not indifferent, nor did he shy away from taking up the cause of his neighbors and countrymen of Galilee. The power in our own teaching is often directly proportionate to the level to which we advance the cause, in our case the gospel cause.

We can never fully appreciate how Jesus did this without knowing a few details about his world and what it was like to be raised and live in rural Galilee in the first century AD. The context of Jesus' social world helps us interpret many of his sayings about the poor or poverty. Some of these teachings may appear difficult to understand without some prior knowledge of his world. One simple example may help demonstrate how historical knowledge will enable us to see the predicaments facing some of Jesus' audiences. For example, a Jewish male in Jesus' day was required to pay an annual temple tax of a half Shekel each year in addition to paying tithes on a variety of household and perishable items (Exodus 33:11ff; 2 Kings 12:5ff). On top of that, each family was taxed according to Roman law. Additional taxes, such as those levied by the Herodians, could be added to that amount, depending on who collected the taxes. This might seem like a somewhat insignificant historical fact, but it is much more than a simple historical piece of information.

From the existing rabbinic evidence, there are hints that some, if not many, Jewish families in Galilee where Jesus taught could not afford to pay both their taxes to the temple and their taxes to Rome and still be able to provide for the needs of a family that relied on agriculture for subsistence. Thus some families were unable to pay their taxes and therefore suffered the consequences, while others were forced to live in near starvation conditions if they made the choice to pay their taxes. In fact, the situation appears to have been so desperate at the time of Jesus that some families would choose to pay their taxes to Rome to avoid imprisonment, but not pay their temple taxes and tithes. As a result of making this decision to befriend Rome and not Judaism, they would be considered unclean or impure, but they would not face imprisonment.[1] In those cases, the poor peasants could be excluded from making offerings at the temple or from having certain ordinances performed for their children such as bar mitzvahs. With two entities—Rome and the temple—pulling from the same limited resources, families had to decide which taxes to pay first. Their choice would determine whether they were imprisoned or whether they were determined clean and upright in their religion. Choosing imprisonment was an impossible solution for many, with no means to provide for a hungry family.

Although we are not certain about Jesus' own financial status, or his particular views on the question of heavy taxation, we do learn that he championed the cause of the poor. His teachings are devoid of positive statements about being rich. Malnutrition, death by starvation, and similar metaphors figure into Jesus' teachings. These themes played to the mentality of the poor and oppressed of Galilee, which made him immensely popular with the common farmers and fishermen living near the Sea of Galilee. In a moment we will consider a few examples where this occurs. In any case, it does seem fairly clear that Jesus taught in a way that suggests a vantage point of the poor or oppressed, and that frequently the rich figure negatively into his parables and teachings.

HOW THE POLITICS OF JESUS' DAY
SHAPED WHAT HE TAUGHT

At the time of Jesus, Galilee and Judea were solidly under the control of Rome and lay on the eastern frontier of the Roman Empire. For this reason and many others, this region of the Roman Empire was important because it acted as a buffer state between the powerful eastern empires and Rome. At the time of Jesus' birth, Galilee and Judea, which both lay on the frontier, were together ruled by a king—Herod the Great—who was placed in power by Roman authorities and who was obligated to be pro-Roman in his outlook. Later in Jesus' life, Judea was ruled by a Roman governor while two of Herod's sons—Herod Antipas and Herod Philip—functioned much like kings and ruled the regions of Galilee and its neighboring territories.

Popular accounts of past generations have made these men out to be harsh, despotic rulers, partially because of their involvement in persecuting Jesus and his family. But for the most part they were no more or less despotic that other rulers of their day.[2] In fact, Philip was a particularly fair and even-handed ruler. Herod Antipas (the Herod mentioned in Matthew 14) was not an especially gifted ruler, but he was not significantly different than his peers, which is likely how we should judge the entire family of Herod rather than comparing them to the great statesmen of the modern era. But what is important for this discussion is how this interplay of Roman governance, local client kings, and burdensome taxation come into play in Jesus' teachings.

As a captive people, the commoners in Galilee and Judea had little or no political voice. They did not choose the Herodian family as their rulers, and they were powerless to resist Roman occupation. They, like Jesus, had opinions about Rome and the Herodian family, but their opinions made little, if any, difference in the way their country was managed. These opinions are expressed in the writings that have survived from those times, such as in the writings of Josephus, who was very pro-Roman, but who at times preserves the antagonism that many of his countrymen felt. Those attitudes are even preserved in the stories of the New Testament. In such a politically charged environment, where the oppressed class seems primed for rebellion, it will be fascinating for us to see whether Jesus was a moderator of the political discussion, a peacemaker, or whether he took a strong, uncompromising viewpoint.

For the most part, the Herodians and a handful of elites dominated the affairs of Galilee and Judea, and the people were powerless to do anything about it. Archeological remains show that the average peasant may have worked and even owned a small plot of land to provide for his family, but those same farmers had very little income beyond the goods that they were able to produce from their farms or perhaps from an acquired skill. Remains of homes within the city walls of rural Galilean towns reveal the foundations of rather small homes, clustered together in small neighborhoods in very tight-knit communities where some homes shared a wall with neighboring homes. Although archeological ruins are famously difficult to understand, the cities that have been uncovered reveal a society of two classes (upper and lower) rather than the typical three-class society of today (upper, middle, and lower).

The lower class was subject to cramped living conditions, food shortages, poor medicine, disease, lack of variety in diet with very little animal protein, and little or no political voice. On the other hand, several estates from the same time period have been uncovered, revealing a very wealthy class of Galileans and Judeans. These estates, that copied the grandeur of the Roman villa in both style and size, were typically owned by out of town or absentee landlords who ran the estates via local overseers.

Suprisingly, these estates begin to appear in the evidence from the Herodian era—Jesus' day—as the chasm between the poor and wealthy increased. In other words, the evidence seems to suggest a growing divide between the rich and poor.

The separation of poor and wealthy in the early period when Herod the Great began to rule was so acute as to create an entire culture of poverty, which resulted in some groups simply packing up their meager belongings and moving to the desert to live with other poor people.[3] The situation was not simply uncomfortable for some of Jesus' peers, many must have considered it dire.

After Rome began ruling and Jews began idealizing the Roman upper class, many farmers lost their land to wealthy estate holders, who made loans to local farmers and then repossessed their land when their crops failed and the farmers failed to pay off loans. Apparently the issue became so acute that a law was passed allowing lenders to still collect their loan payments even in years when the law of Moses traditionally required lenders to forgive all loans. This year, called the year of Jubilee, occurred every seven years (Deuteronomy 15:1–6). The legal exception—the prozbul—permitted the wealthy to still collect on debts owed to them, and was initially created as a help to the poor because the wealthy would not offer loans to the poor in the year or two prior to a Jubilee year. The prozbul was supposed to be a legal loophole permitting the rich to continue to offer loans to the poor, but in reality the poor often defaulted on their loans and without the year of Jubilee their one chance at paying those loans in full became obsolete.

Knowing these historical details of Jesus' society helps us see certain things in his teachings that might not otherwise be obvious. For example, a number of his parables have a rich person in them, a figure that the extremely poor would disdain.

His audiences may have looked to Jesus for solutions or answers to the dawning economic crisis. An important example of how Jesus responded to these concerns can be found in the story of the rich man and Lazarus. The story is told in Luke 16:19–31, and Luke seems to include it as a general teaching of Jesus, rather than as an answer to a specific question. In other words, this teaching in a way personifies Jesus.

It begins with a description of the rich man, who is, "clothed in purple and fine linen, and fared sumptuously every day" (16:19). The normal peasant would never own any article of clothing that was purple because only the richest of the rich could afford it, and in certain contexts only the rich were even permitted to wear it. The dye to produce purple, which was derived from crushing murex shells, was extremely costly, and it is possible that many rural peasants had never even seen true murex-purple cloth. This same man also "fared sumptuously," or in other words, following the Greek text, "he celebrated lavishly every day" of his life (author's translation). This is a far cry from a family who would rarely eat meat and who suffered from malnutrition when the crops do not do well. The rich man in this particular parable is not simply a little better off than the needy poor, he is extremely rich, wearing the colors of a Roman emperor, and eating banquets instead of regular meals.

At this man's house, the beggar Lazarus sits, hoping to receive some handout. A peasant could relate to Lazarus. He has been worn down by extreme malnutrition, and his body is slow in healing itself. He is in such poor shape that, "the dogs came and licked his sores" (16:21). In fact, the Greek text says that Lazarus was, "thrown down" (KJV 16:20 "was laid"). The suggestion is that Lazarus has been thrown down by God or fate, depending on one's personal outlook on life. At this stage, we might ask, about the justice of God and why the poor have been treated so harshly while the rich have been permitted to prosper.[4] According to the parable, both of these men eventually die, and Lazarus goes to Abraham's bosom whereas the rich man goes to Hades. At this stage Jesus' audience would be enjoying a healthy laugh behind their hands at the fate of the rich man, who likely personified the landholders that some of them worked for.

As the story progresses, the rich man, now in hell (or spirit prison following the revelation of the Restoration), asks for certain things from Abraham and Lazarus, specifically that his family will be warned of their wickedness or forgetfulness. Although the theme is certainly implied in the parable, this story is not specifically about missionary work in the world of the spirits, even though Lazarus and the rich man are indeed separated after their deaths. This story is really about the justice of God.

Interestingly, this is the only parable in which Jesus gives his character an actual name. Further, it is the name of one of Jesus' closest followers. Lazarus is extremely poor in this parable, which may in fact have some parallel to Lazarus of Bethany's actual circumstances. Moreover, there is an irony in his name: *Lazarus* means Yahweh helps. The name has the effect of contrast because God is helping Lazarus (the poor) and punishing the rich man who appeared in his life to be blessed. In the eyes of those who heard him speak, and even in our own estimation today, it is easy to assume that God was blessing the rich man and that Lazarus suffered for some sin he had committed.

In the story, the rich man has three requests, and Abraham denies each one of them: "And he cried and said, Father Abraham, have mercy on me, and send Lazarus, that he may dip the tip of his finger in water, and cool my tongue; for I am tormented in this flame" (Luke 16:24). The first two requests are issued as commands or orders. The rich man is still used to giving orders, even though he has died. He has no hesitancy in ordering Abraham around, even when he is in hell and Abraham is in heaven. The second request is for Abraham to send a warning to his family, particularly to his five brothers who still live in their father's mansion. Abraham tells the man that his family already has the law and the prophets, which in this instance is probably included as a great irony.

In reality there is only one sin suggested in the entire story, namely that the rich man has not cared for the poor and the needy. Nothing in the story suggests that the rich man was wicked or that he did anything that would merit being sent to Hades. His sin is rather something that he did *not* do; he neglected to care for the destitute. From the language of the parable, it is possible that Jesus intended the personified rich man to be obedient to the Torah (he realized its importance and wanted his brothers to listen to prophetic counsel), but he had neglected the directive to care for the poor within his gates (see Deuteronomy 15:1–18; Leviticus 25:1–55). The rich man is almost certainly guilty of what Amos taught in Amos 5:12, 15: "they turn aside the poor in the gate from their right. . . . Hate the evil, and love the good, and establish judgment in the gate: it may be that the Lord God of hosts will be gracious unto the remnant of Joseph."

The rich man listens to Abraham's response but then immediately turns to him and tells him that it would be better if he sent Lazarus. The rich man believes that someone from the dead would be able to convince his relatives more quickly to repent, particularly if Abraham would send Lazarus. The man's request shows his deep concern for his family and their welfare even though his state is already miserable. So the rich man is not a completely static, wicked individual; he has some positive attributes also.

Lazarus may be a play on the name Eliezer, who according to rabbinic traditions was sent among the people to see if they were living up to the law (Genesis 15:2).[5] In the end, the powerful teachings that come through in the parable are that God will judge mankind according to all the law, even his directive to care for the poor and the needy; that Lazarus, who appeared to be cursed, was really blessed; and that the rich man, who appeared to be blessed, was really cursed. The poor could relate to this type of parable. They did not even need an explanation or a hint of why the rich man faced such a terrible fate in the afterlife; indeed, they may have expected it. Jesus notes the fate of each man with powerful symbolism, "And it came to pass, that the beggar died, and was carried by the angels into Abraham's bosom: the rich man also died, and was buried" (Luke 16:22). Lazarus was transported into heaven, but the rich man was not going anywhere.

For us there may be something else to glean from the words of this parable and the volatile situation then developing in Galilee and Judea. Certainly the economic and political problems of Jesus' day were not unlike our own. Often, when circumstances seem particularly dire, it is easy to shrug off the situation because our voice may make little, if any, difference. Moreover, when situations such as these develop, it is simple to take the moderate approach, to remain silent on the big issues of the day for fear of offending. Jesus did neither of these things. He spoke to the problems of his day, and in many instances we see that this opinions were incredibly unpopular, causing some to attempt to kill him on the spot while he taught. We also learn that he championed a cause and stood strong by his convictions. Powerful teachers do these very things. They discuss the pertinent issues of the day and they express strong viewpoints that can sometimes cause the wicked to be offended.

THE PRIESTLY CLASS OF JEWS WHO OPPOSED JESUS

Below the Herodian family and Roman governors, local matters in Judea and Galilee were ruled by the elites, primarily the priestly classes of Pharisees and Sadducees. Ruling underneath them were the elders and land owners who were likely the predominant voices in local affairs. One way to see how this system worked is to imagine a fully functioning country with a well-organized civic and religious infrastructure. When the Romans took control of the region, they simply added their taxes and political system directly to the top of the already existing Jewish government (although certainly Jewish governance was also limited). This meant that Judeans and Galileans faced increased taxes and bureaucracy. No one was willing to ease taxes and regulations to make it easier for the newcomer to exist. The Roman policy was to permit local autonomy even if it meant draining the economy to supply its needs.

The priests, particularly the high priest, were in a difficult situation. During and after the reign of Herod the Great, the office of high priest was given as an appointment and later the Roman governors of Judea would actually retain possession of the high priest's robes and would only permit them to be worn on special celebrations. This meant that the high priest would be given the opportunity to celebrate national holidays—ones that were distinctly Jewish and celebrated the goodness of God in delivering his people from Egypt—only after he had asked his Roman conquerors for permission to wear the sacred vestments. Moreover, a Roman garrison protected the temple precincts. In many ways, this type of control would create a collection of leaders who had something to prove, who needed to demonstrate their power despite the controls being placed on them.

The important point to note, however, is not the economic or civic structure of Galilee or Judea, but what it meant for a popular teacher like Jesus. We have already seen where some of his teachings expressed the mentality of the poor in a society with an increasing economic divide. He was overwhelmingly popular with the crowds, particularly the people from the small rural towns of Galilee, but not with the elites. On the other hand, his teachings that contain references to the causes of the poor would not necessarily make him unpopular among the rulers of the Jews. They may also have disliked Roman leadership or burdensome taxation. If Jesus did indeed champion the cause of the poor, then his popularity among them is certainly understandable, but a further look into his teaching will be necessary to discover what made him so unpopular among another class of society: the priests and elders.

For many reasons, the success and popularity of the rich may have been tied to the causes of the poor, particularly in the political arena outside of Judea because their fortunes were so intertwined. Nearly without exception, the elders, chief priests, scribes, and other elites eventually came to hate him. (Nicodemus was one of the few notable exceptions.) Some Pharisees later joined the church (Acts 15:3), but for the most part the relationship between Jesus and the elites was confrontational.

To explain why he evoked such a negative reaction from this segment of society, it is not enough to simply state that he sided with one group. He went beyond expressing the opinions of the poor. He, at times, needled and criticized the elite, religious leaders. One example might show how this was carried out, and it again demonstrates his willingness to take up a cause and speak against certain injustices. Jesus taught a parable sometimes referred to as the Parable of the Wicked Husbandmen shortly after his triumphal entry into the city of Jerusalem. In it he perfectly describes the social situation of Galilee and Judea at the time, a position that again would have been highly popular with the peasantry, but in this case also highly objectionable to the ruling classes. He began by telling a story of a landowner who rented his land to distant husbandmen. The husbandmen immediately get behind in their rent, possibly because they were greedy and refused to pay. The landowner, being patient, sent someone to check on their status and receive the rent due to him. Surprisingly, the husbandmen mistreat the messengers and eventually kill several of them (Mark 12:5). At this point, we ask, "What type of indulgent landowner would continue to look the other way despite such despicable behavior?" These husbandmen are clearly criminals who have stolen land that did not belong to them and are trying to glut themselves rent-free on someone else's land.

We might rightly ask why the landowner would eventually send his son to the vineyard and endanger his son's life when his tenants have already mistreated his messengers so shamefully. In fact, they killed some of the servants, which would certainly cause a landowner to worry about the life of his son.

In a way, the parable is a trap. By making the landowner, who certainly symbolizes God the Father, so absolutely indulgent and longsuffering, Jesus has made the answer to the riddle blatantly obvious, almost too obvious. Jesus continues by relating how the landowners take the son and kill him, which begs the question of why they would kill the owner's son. Certainly the renters did not suppose that they could kill all of the landowner's servants and his heir and thereby possess the land for themselves.

Jesus then turned and asks his audience (the elites, not the poor), "What shall therefore the lord of the vineyard do?" (Mark 12:9). The answer is so obvious that no one really needed to vocalize it. The husbandmen deserve to receive the full punishment that the law can provide. Interestingly Jesus' opponents seem to know right away that he was speaking about them. But how would they know this? He had not mentioned anyone's name, nor had he implied that the wicked tenets were Sadducees, Pharisees, or even Jews for that matter. The story could relate practices resulting from Roman domination, but the Gospels are unanimous in testifying that the Jewish elite thought he was speaking of them.

This is where the social context makes the meaning of the parable more profound. If we simply substitute the Herodians, wealthy estate holders, or elites for the husbandmen; God in place of the landowner; and the prophets in place of the messengers, then we begin to see what was going on in Galilee and Judea at the time. The ruling classes were dominating the economy of the region and overlooking the poor, over whom God had specifically given them charge (Amos 8:4–7; Deuteronomy 15:7, 11). Moreover, the indulgent landowner (the Lord) would eventually set his affairs in order, and from the context of the parable, it appears that he may have already waited much longer than anyone would expect him to wait.

Any peasant in Jesus' audience would have recognized the parody being made of the ruling elite. It was clear to them what was happening, and somehow it was also clear to the wealthy. Specifically, the reason the Father acts with so much indulgence and patience in this particular parable is in part to amplify the expectation of the crowd to look forward to the time when God would punish the wicked. The parable envisions a situation so dire that God would certainly remedy it soon—even the elites had to agree with Jesus on that point. Those who heard it may have realized that the death of the son was the trigger for the remedy, and thus their hope may have turned to Jesus. But the parable also helps us see beyond the adoration of Jesus' followers to a group of antagonists whom Jesus prodded and offended publicly (Matthew 21:45–46).

In the first section of this chapter we saw that Jesus was willing to champion difficult causes and to discuss matters that were of incredible popular interest. In the first story, the rich man is a metaphor for the dominant ruling classes, but apparently no one specifically assumed that Jesus was referring to them. Instead, the parable described conditions in Judea and Galilee generally. In this second example, Jesus offered a more public rebuke at a moment when some already wanted to kill him for the implications of his triumphal entry into Jerusalem. Some people thought that he was directly accusing or parodying them. Certainly he was not afraid to teach in challenging situations and to express his opinions clearly, even when they were unpopular.

Holiness and Uncleanness:
Justification versus Sanctification

Apart from the fact that the Gospel authors describe Jesus as the spokesman for the poor, there was an issue that further divided Jesus from his opponents. Certainly Jesus may have offered pointed rebukes or even have publicly showed up his opponents in front of their peers, but it is still possible that the elites could have waved off those challenges as unfounded or ridiculous. They could have taken the criticism in stride. But something in his teachings and general outlook was so different from their own that it was impossible to ever resolve their differences without one side completely accepting the views of the other. A compromise seemed out of the question.

To appreciate that fundamental difference, what it meant for Jesus, and what it means for us today, it is important to first see the problem in its historical context. That great difference, the issue that could not be resolved without significant repentance, was the underlying understanding of what it means to be holy or pure. The struggle that existed between Jesus and his enemies was that even though they were all obedient to the same laws, namely the law of Moses, they interpreted those laws differently. In other words, Jesus' opponents were not advocates of disobedience to the law; rather they rejected Jesus' interpretation of what it meant to be righteous. Even though both parties adhered to the law of Moses, they both also seem to have considered the other unclean, impure, wicked, and unrighteous. Certainly we must side with Jesus in this debate as we read about the murderous attempts of Jesus' opponents and their hardheartedness, but the gospels also record accusations from leading Jews of Jesus breaking the law.

For the Jews, the important question was whether we are considered holy because we obey every aspect or letter of the law, or whether we are holy because we have pure hearts and obey the commandments. In other words, is it enough to simply live the commandments? Certainly some of Jesus' enemies were hardhearted and some of them he denounced for their wickedness, but in the majority of the debates between Jesus and his contemporaries there is no mention of sin on the part of the accusers. Instead, it often came down to personal interpretations of law. Unfortunately, we often assume that because Jesus taught kindness, the Jews were somehow hardhearted, or since Jesus taught Christians to be obedient, the

Jews were disobedient. The issue in Jesus' day was a matter of emphasis not disobedience. The Jews believed God had revealed the law that they sought to obey.[6] One of the great misconceptions about Judaism at the time of Jesus is the idea that the Jews were an utterly corrupt and fallen people. There were many good people living in Jesus' day, and those were just among the rulers of the Jews. The Jews were an obedient people and they loved God.

Fortunately, using modern terminology we can distinguish between the two methods of thinking: defining holiness as obedience to every aspect of the law and defining it as the pure in heart. Justification relates to a person who has lived up to the entire law and who has been obedient to the commandments in all their particulars. That person is justified, or made just (from the Latin iustus meaning "just, upright, righteous in accordance with law"[7]). On the other hand, sanctification emanates from the inside out; it is a way of being. A person who has pure motives, a pure heart, and clean thoughts is sanctified. This person is holy through and through. It is possible to be justified but not be sanctified. This appears to be one of Jesus' core teachings, although the opposite does not appear possible (to be sanctified and not justified), or at least it is never exemplified in scripture (Matthew 23:27–28).

Some of Jesus' contemporaries were so obedient to the law that they constructed extra ways of obeying the commandments. For example, the Pharisees symbolically constructed a fence around the law so that no one would even come close to breaking those commandments. In essence, a person would automatically break a lesser commandment before they could break one of the commandments of God. It was a safety net. The Pharisees were absolutely obedient to the commandments. And although there were corrupt leaders among them, that problem was not unique to the Pharisees.

On the other hand, the Sadducees were more strictly rigid in their approach to the law. They accepted the law of Moses as the prophet had revealed it, and the later prophets were viewed as a corollary to or commentary on the law. The prophets and history books of the Old Testament revealed their inspired history, but the law was the pinnacle of all of God's teachings.

They, the Sadducees, did not believe in a personal individual existence after death, which meant that they did not use the fear of punishment in the afterlife as a motivation to be obedient. Instead, they believed that

God loved them and chose them, and as a result of this way of thinking they may have struggled with elitism. They made concessions to Rome to maintain their position of authority, but they were likewise rigidly obedient to the law of God. For the most part, they seem to have controlled the temple and the Sanhedrin in Jesus' day.

Interestingly, Jesus had most of his negative encounters with the Pharisees, but it was likely the Sadducees who orchestrated his arrest and delivery to Pilate. (There is only one mention of the Pharisees' involvement in Jesus' death, and it occurs after Jesus entered Gethsemane.) This happened for a number of significant reasons. First, the Sadducees had greater political control in Judea, where Jesus was crucified, which meant that it would have been difficult for the Pharisees to carry out Jesus' arrest without any Sadducean involvement. Second, the Sadducees in Galilee did not engage in the doctrinal controversies to the same extent that the Pharisees did. They may have done so in Judea, but Jesus did not visit Judea often. Therefore they would have had few opportunities to dispute Jesus' teachings. Third, for the most part, the Sadducees remained exclusively in Judea.

Considering the social setting for a moment, we are able to see a number of important points of emphasis in Jesus' teachings and how his awareness of each audience and topic shaped his teachings. Frequently, Jesus was challenged on matters of personal interpretation of scripture as well as rigid interpretation of the law. Indeed, some Jews believed his healing miracles to be acts of work or they believed that Jesus spoke irreverently or in a way that was blasphemous (John 9:14–16; 10:30–31). In those moments of accusation and confrontation Jesus could have responded to his accusers using the same language of challenge and accusation. Paul used the tensions and differences of belief between the Pharisees and Sadducees to cause discord to arise between them and thus turn away their wrath from his own situation (Acts 23:6–8). Jesus, on the other hand, often responded to those situations by teaching truth. Confrontational words were not typically part of his vocabulary, although we have seen in the two previous examples that he did not shy away from difficult and potentially unpopular discussions.[8]

Another important issue arising out of these considerations is that it now appears obvious that either the masses assumed Jesus was a Pharisee or the Pharisees themselves thought that Jesus was a Pharisee. In the New Testament this assumption is often revealed in the stories where people thought that Jesus should have been obedient to the laws of the Pharisees when he was not (for example, Matthew 12:1–9). Jesus was not typically accused of breaking the law of Moses (the accusations of blasphemy may be an exception to this), but rather of breaking the Pharisaic interpretation of the law. In many of those instances when Jesus is accused of violating Pharisaic procedures or thinking, the Pharisees are not even mentioned as being present (for example, John 5:1–10). It may be that the common people perceived him to be a Pharisee, but no one seems to have ever thought that Jesus was a Sadducee.

An important point concerning audience arises out of this occurrence. In teaching the gospel, Jesus likely encountered numerous people who held wrong or misguided opinions about him. They may have been slightly wrong concerning his intentions and purpose, or in some cases even drastically wrong. Rather than point out the distinct differences and offer pointed clarification of what made his teachings unique (which would have been a great help today), Jesus let those misunderstandings simmer. Perhaps he saw the potential for growth in allowing those points of ambiguity to remain or perhaps he had other reasons for not pointing out the differences.

There is an instance when the Sadducees questioned Jesus about a certain doctrine. In that instance, it is apparent that they believed Jesus would offer a Pharisaic interpretation to their riddle. However, he caught them off guard with his response, which neither follows typical Pharisaic thinking nor traditional Sadducean thinking on the issue (Matthew 22:23–33).

That Jesus had some affinities with the Pharisees, or at least some supposed affinities with the Pharisees, helps explain why there were so many requests for him to clarify the differences between his teachings and those of the Pharisees. But in all of the stories that are preserved about Jesus, there are no hints that Jesus had any ties to the ruling elite. He is always depicted as an outsider to their laws and ways of life, and they appear to consistently be his antagonists. He was not their equal as far as family, authority, prestige, or honor were concerned; at least in their eyes they assumed that he did not have the proper authority, family ties, or prestige.

Perhaps more important, the gospels do not record that Jesus ever pointed out that he was not a Pharisee and was not obligated to follow their ways of thinking or their particular interpretations. He easily could have rebuked the Pharisees for even assuming that he would follow their oral traditions. Instead he was careful to respond while at the same time building a clear picture of his own ministry using the Son of Man title to explain what he had come to do. His ministry was to draw all mankind to him, and a confrontational ministry that was filled with angry words and divisive speeches apparently would not have achieved the results he desired. Jesus faced severe criticism for what he taught, and his own ideas were the subject of public ridicule, making him very much like us.

Like other societies where the ruling elite dominate government, the economy, and other public affairs, Jesus lived in a society where life was difficult for the poor, and their voice was not heard. History is filled with stories of individuals who reacted to such oppression and subjugation. But rather than speak out against such a system as others in his day did, Jesus quietly and humbly taught the gospel of salvation. The great irony is that he was the king of Israel, the anointed one; and he had a legitimate claim to govern. Speaking out against Rome and Judean corruption may have made him wildly popular with masses, but he remained focused on his mission. And even when the opportunity arose to evoke controversy among the elite, he remained poised and delivered his message. In the end, his teachings and practices appealed to the poor and represented an ideology that pleased those who were searching for deliverance. That deliverance came through Jesus' peaceful life and the humble words he spoke, rather than through conflict. But it is equally important to note that Jesus sometimes challenged his accusers, not with accusation or boisterous claims, but by criticizing their practices openly, thus putting them to shame. As a teacher he demonstrated both styles of teaching: appealing to the neglected and at times challenging the oppressors.

SUMMARY

In a society governed by a foreign power and caught up in a climate of religious zeal, Jesus could have taught the gospel in a variety of ways. Great social reformers have always found a way of expressing themselves to one class of people while searching for change in another. For Jesus, those he reached out to were the socially marginalized and oppressed, and he called for change among those who had power to make change. He did not, however, critique Roman domination of Judea and Galilee (at least as far as the Gospels authors remembered). Rather, he called on religious leaders to renew their obedience to the law of Moses and consider lessening their trend toward rigidity in living that law. When doing so, he often used strong language. He told his disciples that God would punish the unrepentant and he prophesied of the coming of the Kingdom of God.

While carrying out this criticism of certain Jewish leaders, Jesus also taught a message of peace to the poor and those who accepted him and followed him. He taught parables about the poor and how they would be blessed in the hereafter, while the hardhearted (personified at times as the rich) would be punished. He defined holiness as an inner quality. This went against the views of his contemporaries who often focused on obedience to physical commandments as the primary indicator of righteousness. He frequently avoided the great debates of the day between the Pharisees and Sadducees, and it appears that even though they at times attempted to draw him into their conflicts, he remained focused on his message and ministry, while at the same time teaching the eternal truths the Father had entrusted to him to teach.

At the heart of this attribute of Jesus' teaching style was his ability to engage two different groups at the same time, one positively and one negatively, but we cannot simply make Jesus out to be a champion of the oppressed. His teaching style was broader than that, encompassing all levels of Judean society but largely excluding the issue of Rome and Roman domination. In our own teaching, if we are to follow Jesus in this attribute, we might seek to engage a broader audience, but also remember to champion the causes of the Lord and his gospel while seeking change in that broader context.

ATTRIBUTE 2

Using Proverbs and Wisdom in Teaching

Jesus' Original Proverbs or Wisdom Sayings at a Glance:

- "Let the dead bury their dead: but go thou and preach the kingdom of God" (Luke 9:60).
- "But I say unto you, That ye resist not evil; but whosoever shall smite thee on thy right cheek, turn to him the other also" (Matthew 5:39).
- "It is more blessed to give than to receive" (Acts 20:35).
- "But many that are first shall be last; and the last first" (Mark 10:31).
- "No man, having put his hand to the plough, and looking back, is fit for the kingdom of God" (Luke 9:62).
- "For whosoever exalteth himself shall be abased; and he that humbleth himself shall be exalted" (Luke 14:11).
- "It is easier for a camel to go through the eye of a needle, than for a rich man to enter into the kingdom of God" (Mark 10:25).

Understanding the World from Jesus' Perspective: Proverbs and Wisdom

So many modern studies on the life of Jesus have focused on describing Jesus' world through the eyes of his contemporaries, an exercise that is often quite valuable and insightful. But unfortunately those same studies cannot tell us how Jesus saw his world. He may have had opinions similar to those expressed by others or he could have held radically differing viewpoints. In fact, from the descriptions of his life in the four Gospels, we might suspect that he saw the world in a way that was fundamentally different from his contemporaries. Perhaps Jesus felt oppressed by Roman rule or perhaps he felt that Roman taxation was a burden upon poor Galileans as some in his day felt, but perhaps he also endorsed the practice as a means of maintaining peace and stability in an otherwise tumultuous region of the world. Others of his day avoided doctors because patients often went home worse than they were before their first visit. Did Jesus feel that way? Rather than look at Jesus' day through the eyes of others and then assume that Jesus held similar opinions, we might look into his teachings and see the ways that he described the world around him. His proverbs are one such window into this world.

Students often remember best those teachers who use proverbs or witty sayings in their presentations. Benjamin Franklin, for example, was particularly fond of using proverbs in his public speeches, and some of them have become almost legendary—"Visitors are like fish, after three days they stink." Jesus was also fond of using proverbs in his teachings. Today many of them are not remembered specifically as proverbs, yet a small number of his sayings are indeed remembered as being proverbial. Consider for example the following proverbs of Jesus: "It is more blessed to give than to receive" (Acts 20:35) or "Take therefore no thought for the morrow: for the morrow shall take thought for the things of itself. Sufficient unto the day is the evil thereof" (Matthew 6:34). The wording of both of these proverbs seems to originate with Jesus and is not simply a common proverb of his day that he drew upon to give depth and diversity to his own teachings.

Proverbs are catchy in part because they are poetic descriptions of life generally and human existence specifically. Proverbial bits of wisdom also provide the listener something that can easily be remembered, something that can be readily repeated and passed on. Jesus often drew on proverbs, some of them already circulating in his day and others unique to him. In a largely oral culture, proverbs provide a teacher with a means of giving his or her listeners something to remember easily. One reason for looking at the proverbs or wise sayings of Jesus is that he drew on a number of themes from his daily life that help us in turn gain a greater appreciation of who he was and what he was like in his mortal lifetime. They can also inform us about his environment and the injustices or social issues to which he drew his audiences' attention.

The Proverbs of Jesus

Jesus drew upon a number of important themes in his proverbs, namely local physicians, prophets, and the power of Satan. He also drew upon physical images familiar to his audiences such as birds, foxes, sparrows, sheep, wolves, snakes, dogs, and lilies. And he drew on images that were likely unfamiliar to his Jewish audiences such as pigs. Many of his proverbs contain references to common occupations such as farming, harvesting, and tending vineyards. On occasion he even spoke of having a sliver in one's eye and building a house on a sandy foundation, images that may have derived directly from his occupation (Mark 6:3). Although the list of things that he did not mention in his proverbs could become enormous, it is interesting that items associated with wealth are mentioned only negatively, leisure time is also foreign to his teachings, as is travel and other things associated typically with the wealthy.

Images and descriptions of rural farm life reach back into the world of Jesus and reveal a man who grew up in a working class environment and who drew on ideas and concepts associated particularly with farm life in first century Galilee. In his parables he often spoke of the rich or the ruling classes of chief priests and Herodians, but the common wisdom he drew upon reveals a decidedly peasant background. Riches, landlords, and luxury are often spoken of with disdain in Jesus' teachings. In other words, he saw life from a peasant's standpoint rather than from the viewpoint of the rich ruling class, which interestingly coincides with his teachings on poverty that we have seen already.

From his surviving proverbs and wise sayings, it is apparent that Jesus was also quite rigorous in his outlook, showing that he could offer strong public rebukes and ask poignant and cutting questions: in other words, he seems to have advocated the mentality of the working class rather than simply being an outside admirer of it. He also drew out strong contrasts between what some individuals perceived to be truth and eternal reality. One of his most descriptive examples comes from the Gospel of Luke where Jesus says, "No man, having put his hand to the plough, and looking back, is fit for the kingdom of God" (Luke 9:62).

To help us gain something meaningful from Jesus' proverbs and learn what it indicates about teaching style, it is important to understand how he used them and how they have survived. First of all, we need to remember that the sayings of Jesus that have survived are the ones that were remembered or were memorable. Certainly he said many things that no one recorded or remembered. Many of his proverbs, in particular, have a strong popular appeal because they drew on common assumptions or contemporary wisdom. The proverb preserved in Luke 9:62 (mentioned on the previous page) draws on language that was familiar to Jesus' Galilean audiences, capturing the very popular concept that hard work is expected of those who enter the kingdom. Farming was among the most labor intensive occupations of the pre-industrialized world, and with this proverb Jesus helps his local peasant audience—who were probably all farmers or benefited directly from farming—see that hard work is a valuable asset for those who would desire to enter the kingdom of God. He was not trying to make his message appealing to wealthy aristocrats, but to common hard-working people who had sunburned brows. By contrast, when Paul discussed the same subject, he used theological terms like *grace, faith,* and *salvation.*

Jesus' proverbs contain many other details from his personal surroundings that help the modern reader see the setting in which he lived. Farming imagery is prevalent in Jesus' proverbs and parables. For example, he was familiar with wine and storing it (Mark 2:22), the number of laborers required to manage a harvest (Matthew 9:37), and placing a candle underneath a harvest basket (Mark 4:21).

Animal imagery also figures into his teachings. He taught about feeding dogs and swine (Matthew 7:6) and he described the apostles' ministry as being like sheep among wolves (Matthew 10:16). In the latter teaching, he also encouraged the disciples to be "wise as serpents, and harmless as doves" (Matthew 10:16). On the same occasion, he also taught a second proverb drawing upon bird imagery: "Are not two sparrows sold for a farthing? and one of them shall not fall on the ground without your Father" (Matthew 10:28–31).

On two other occasions he used animal imagery in his proverbs. When speaking to the young, rich man who wanted to know which commandments he should emphasize or re-emphasize in his obedience, Jesus drew upon one of the most extreme images ever presented in all of his teachings. Jesus taught him that it would be easier for a camel to pass through the eye of a sewing needle than for a rich man to make it into heaven. The camel is the largest land mammal living in the holy land, and the thought of it being pushed through the eye of a common sewing needle is indeed striking. Modern attempts to find some way around the stark contrast presented in this parable have proven fruitless. Archaeologists have never uncovered a gate into Jerusalem that was referred to as the "eye of the needle" and that was used for camels to pass through the city wall; the supposed confusion between the word camel and rope in the story would imply that Jesus was speaking Greek and his disciples who recorded the story did not understand his words.[1] These images place Jesus in a society that was familiar with pack animals and sewing needles. Later in his ministry, the Lord drew upon another startling image: "For wheresoever the carcass is, there will the eagles [vultures] be gathered together" (Matthew 24:28).[2] The idea is uncommon in urban settings, but in rural communities, vultures picking apart a carcass are not out of the ordinary. In addition to the everyday life imagery preserved from rural Galilee, we also see that Jesus was fond of using contrasts or hyperbole to teach the gospel.

All of these images describe a typical rural setting for Jesus and his disciples. His followers understood farming and harvest time as well as animals and animal husbandry. Nazareth and Capernaum are very small cities, and the few disciples whose hometowns are mentioned also come from very small, rural towns. For example, Peter, Andrew, and Philip all came from a fishing village named Bethsaida (John 1:44; 12:21). Nathanael came from a very small village named Cana (John 21:2). In fact, the two major cities in Galilee—Sepphoris and Tiberias—are never mentioned as places where Jesus ministered and taught the gospel. Perhaps Jesus stayed in the smaller towns and villages and avoided the large cities whenever possible, choosing instead to teach the gospel among other rural communities. In fact, the cities he visited and spoke of often typically had populations in the hundreds rather than thousands.

Clearly Jesus' physical surroundings, his upbringing in a rural Galilean farming community, and popular concerns shaped the way he delivered the message. Rather than longing for the training of the Rabbis or the grandeur of academic training in Rome or Greece, Jesus embraced his upbringing and education and passed on the life lessons he had learned to his audiences. His perspective could at times be strong and demanding, but it resonated with the rural audiences who heard him speak.

Some Possible Personal Viewpoints of Jesus

Jesus grew up and lived in a society where medicine was more magic than science, and where being healed through medicine was more luck than skill. Some surgeries were perfected in the Roman era, and shortly after Jesus, a Roman doctor named Galen (AD 129–200) successfully performed a brain surgery where the patient survived. Other archaeological discoveries show that some advances were being made, but for the most part, rural citizens were very skeptical of doctors. Among Greeks, it was popular for the sick to travel to a shrine dedicated to the pagan god Asclepius and seek the help of doctors there. At these shrines, doctors would direct the afflicted to spend a night or several nights in an incubation room where they were sometimes surrounded by snakes and other crawling things. Other reports seem to presuppose the use of hallucinogenic drugs to aid the healing process. It is no wonder that many of Jesus' contemporaries were skeptical about doctors and medicine.

A similar skepticism seems to come through in one of Jesus' proverbs. Jesus said, "They that are whole have no need of a physician, but they that are sick" (Mark 2:17). The saying seems to hint that one should not consider visiting a doctor unless one is genuinely sick, in other words preventive medicine was not encouraged. There was no need to chance becoming worse off at the hands of a doctor if one was not truly ill. Interestingly, the same statement does not hold true today. Jesus' words tell us something about *his* day. Mark expresses most succinctly the skepticism many felt about physicians, "And [she] had suffered many things of many physicians, and had spent all that she had, and was nothing bettered, *but rather grew worse*" (Mark 5:26; emphasis added).

On another occasion, Jesus shows his familiarity with the effects of robbery. In fact, he used the image of robbery to teach a truth: "No man can enter into a strong man's house, and spoil his goods, except he will first bind the strong man; and then he will spoil his house" (Mark 3:27).[3] Although Jesus used the image to describe the overthrow and binding of Satan, it does tell us something of his world—a world in which robbery or the threat of it was familiar. His audiences lived in a time when insurance companies did not replace personal belongings after a theft; therefore, a robbery could leave a family absolutely desolate. In the modern world, robbery is often an inconvenience, but in Jesus' day it could completely destroy a home and family. This image made sense to his audiences who had no standing guards at their homes, and who could not afford to lose their belongings. Therefore the ruin that Satan could cause was similar to robbery in his day, but it is very different from the effects of robbery today.

One of the most dramatic differences between Jesus' teachings and the practices of our day comes in the form of a proverb. He taught, "Agree with thine adversary quickly, whiles thou art in the way with him; lest at any time the adversary deliver thee to the judge, and the judge deliver thee to the officer, and thou be cast into prison. Verily I say unto thee, Thou shalt by no means come out thence, till thou hast paid the uttermost farthing" (Matthew 5:25–26). The intent of this saying is to encourage his followers to settle their disputes out of court, a point that Paul also encouraged (1 Corinthians 6:1–9). Whether this is even possible in the modern era is an important question, but Jesus encouraged his followers to settle their disputes quickly and outside the established court system probably because in the end those who pursue court-mediated decisions may end up worse off. One reason for this may be the fact that many Jews viewed Roman courts as illegitimate and an imposition upon God's people.[4]

The courts he was speaking of could have been either Roman or Jewish, but given the monetary overtones of the saying and the fact that imprisonment could result from the dispute, his audiences would likely have thought of a Roman court. A local Jewish court made up of the elders of the community could not send a person to prison. This saying opens up the tantalizing possibility that Jesus had concerns about the justice of the Roman system in Judea and Galilee, and encouraged his followers to steer clear of it whenever possible.

A few of Jesus' surviving proverbs reveal a very strong and powerful side to his personality, which may initially appear to contradict what we think of as meek. In the modern era, one of the most common character traits attributed to Jesus is meekness, yet when we look at the Gospels we are surprised to find that only the Gospel of Matthew says that Jesus was meek (Matthew 11:29; 21:5); the other New Testament writers did not refer to him in that way. Ironically, the adjective "humble" is never used in reference to Jesus in the New Testament, even though we often think of him as humble, meek, and submissive. The following passages do not typically come to mind when we think of the meekness of the Savior, but instead they show a stronger side of his character. That is not to suggest that Jesus was not meek, or that he was not humble, but only that the four Gospel writers did not typically refer to him using those adjectives. Rather, they thought of him as powerful and strong.

Early in Jesus' ministry, while he taught in Galilee, a certain scribe came to Jesus and asked if he could become a follower of Jesus. Jesus responded to him favorably while reflecting on Jesus' own difficult physical circumstances (Matthew 8:18–20). Matthew then immediately connects the story of "another of his disciples" who asked Jesus if he could take time to bury his father (Matthew 8:21). The two stories seem to be a contrast in types of discipleship. The first request came from a scribe who had not previously followed Jesus. The second request came from someone who was already identified as a disciple but who allowed certain (legitimate) temporal concerns to get in the way of following Jesus. To the second request, Jesus answered in a way that seems abrupt and terse. He told the second questioner, "Follow me; and let the dead bury their dead" (Matthew 8:22). Perhaps some part of this proverb is missing that would make the account seem less abrasive to modern sensibilities, but it still shows a very demanding side of Jesus' personality.[5]

Another of Jesus' proverbs shows an equally strong side of his character. During the Sermon on the Mount, Jesus taught a group of followers what he would ask of his disciples. Following the order of the story as the Gospel of Matthew tells it, Jesus had recently called four disciples prior to delivering the Sermon on the Mount. Possibly those four—Peter, Andrew, James, and John—had already committed their lives to Jesus and had left behind their jobs, but Matthew does not explicitly state that they had done so. Instead, Matthew reports that they "left their nets, and followed him" (Matthew 4:20) and that James and John, "immediately left the ship and their father, and followed him" (Matthew 4:22). Certainly, one of the implications of these two statements is that they left their jobs permanently. Because the disciples later returned to their jobs (John 21:2–6), it is possible that they did maintain some ties to their work throughout their public ministry.

To a small group of such disciples and followers, Jesus asked them to make a monumental sacrifice *prior* to officially calling them as apostles. In words that are now proverbial, Jesus asked them to, "Take no thought for your life, what ye shall eat, or what ye shall drink; nor yet for your body, what ye shall put on. . . . Wherefore, if God so clothe the grass of the field, which to day is, and to morrow is cast into the oven, shall he not much more clothe you, O ye of little faith?" (Matthew 6:25, 30). Jesus asked each of them to make what would likely be the greatest temporal sacrifice of their lives. He asked them each to leave their worldly cares behind and follow him, with the implication that God would take care of their temporal needs. Some of them may have felt uneasy at giving up their temporal safety net, but at least twelve of those early disciples came forward to follow him. The call that Jesus extended to those early followers shows how demanding Jesus could be of his followers. This call in our own day has only been extended to a select few and not to the membership of the Church generally. Jesus asked his disciples to give up their jobs to serve him, but as far as our records indicate, only a select group accepted that difficult call. Moreover, Jesus seems to have followed that same advice. He did not work during his public ministry; he relied on faithful followers to provide for his needs (Luke 8:1–3).

Also in the context of the Sermon on the Mount, Jesus taught those same disciples to "Love your enemies, bless them that curse you, do good to them that hate you, and pray for them which despitefully use you, and persecute you" (Matthew 5:44). Even though this proverb, taken together with the proverb concerning clothing and temporal needs, may be classified as part of the eternal gospel that Jesus was sent to teach, these teachings would have a powerful impact on those who were called to live them. They were being asked to forget about what they would wear and focus instead on loving those who would hate them, suggesting that Jesus anticipated that his message would draw a negative reaction from some. These men were not being called into a service where they would grow rich and prosper financially, but rather they were called to forego certain luxuries and instead focus on the internal struggle of loving those who would persecute them.

One element of Jesus' teaching style that rises to the surface as we study his life is that he was serious about what discipleship would mean. He did not ask for interest or empathy only, but for genuine commitment and lifelong discipleship. Such a message may have made him seem demanding, but many were willing to accept the call.

Proverbs That May Reveal Jesus' Emotions

Several of Jesus' proverbial teachings reveal something of his own concerns and thoughts about life in general. From one of his earliest teachings, Jesus told a gathering in his hometown that, "No prophet is accepted in his own country" (Luke 4:24) after a group of listeners in the local synagogue rejected him for alluding to the possibility that he was the literal fulfillment of Isaiah 61:1–2. The Gospel of Mark adds a slightly different version of the saying, but places it in the same context that Luke did. He reports that Jesus said, "A prophet is not without honor, but in his own country, and among his own kin, and in his own house" (Mark 6:4).

Whether Luke or Mark more accurately preserves exactly what Jesus said is difficult to know, although Luke's statement is more proverbial, while Mark's shows greater personal introspection. Luke never introduces Jesus' siblings by name into his story, but in the verse preceding Jesus' statement concerning the rejection of prophets in their hometowns Mark reports that Jesus had four brothers—James, Joses, Juda, and Simon— and at least two sisters (Mark 6:3). Unlike Luke's account where Jesus is rejected in his hometown, Mark links the statement directly to Jesus' family. In Mark's words, "A prophet is not without honor, but *in his own country, and among his own kin, and in his own house*" (emphasis added); in other words, a prophet does receive honor, except among his own countrymen, among his relatives, and in his own house. Mark does not specifically say that Jesus' family rejected or accepted his teachings, but he certainly implies that Jesus did not receive honor among his local peers (his own country), among his peers in Nazareth (his own kin), or even among the members of his own family (his own house). The saying could be rendered more literally, "A prophet is not without honor, except among his countrymen, his own relatives, and in his own house." The Gospel of Mark certainly implies that some of Jesus' family and relatives rejected him, while the Gospel of John teaches that Jesus' siblings were openly antagonistic to him (John 7:1–5).[6]

This proverb reveals some of the personal anguish that Jesus experienced in his mortal ministry when members of his own family and hometown rejected his claim to be the Messiah. In reality, the saying directly reflects an experience opposite that of the prophet Amos, who was accepted in his own town but rejected in other towns in northern Israel (Amos 7:10–13). The saying itself is not a static eternal truth because our own prophets are accepted completely and openly among Latter-day Saints (i.e. in their hometowns) but often rejected outside of the community of saints. Jesus found the opposite to be true: that is, his own people and some of his own family members rejected him, but at the same time the saying implies that he would find acceptance elsewhere ("A prophet is not without honor"). However, Jesus did not find wide acceptance in Judea, although some did accept him in Galilee.

Another similar proverbial saying shows an equally reflective side of Jesus. He said, "The foxes have holes, and the birds of the air have nests; but the Son of man hath not where to lay his head" (Matthew 8:20). Certainly the title "Son of man" refers to Jesus himself and reflects the homelessness of the Savior in this particular saying. Whether this was physical or emotional homelessness is still an open question today, but the proverb begins by describing the physical situation of two animals common to Galilee, which may indicate that Jesus intended it to be understood literally. In other words, Jesus appears to long for shelter in this saying, hoping to have a place to lay his head. The Gospels are unclear whether Jesus ever owned a home during his mortal ministry, but a few ambiguous statements in the Gospels may be interpreted to mean that Jesus did own a house, particularly during the early parts of his ministry. The KJV translation may be influenced, in part, by the idea that because Jesus' disciples had given all to follow him, Jesus also had given all away. Mark, however, records that while at Capernaum, "it was reported that he was at home" (Mark 2:1; NRSV) although John records that Andrew and another disciple visited Jesus while he was staying with someone: "They said to him 'Rabbi' (which translated means Teacher), 'where are you staying?' He said to them, 'Come and see'" (John 1:38–39; NRSV). The question of whether he owned a home or stayed with various people throughout his life is still open, but the proverb shows that he longed for a permanent place to stay. There may also be a symbolic reference to the state of the temple in Jesus' day, when it had deviated from the spiritual sanctuary it was designed to be. If this is so, then Jesus' homelessness or longing for a permanent home may also reflect his concern for the loss of the temple as a spiritual sanctuary for the pure.

As the ministry progressed, Jesus became increasingly unwelcome in Judea (John 7:1; 11:7–9, 16) as hostile forces began to coalesce and his opponents sought to take his life. Certainly this opposition must have taken its toll on Jesus, both physically and emotionally. And on occasion he may have felt that rejection in a way that led him to exclaim that he had nowhere safe to lay his head at night. Even though some showed him hospitality (Luke 8:1–3; 19:2–8), he felt rejection and expressed those feelings on a number of occasions.

Another personal concern of the Lord can be seen in his proverb about children. Shortly after the experiences on the Mount of Transfiguration, Jesus said, "And whosoever shall offend one of these little ones that believe in me, it is better for him that a millstone were hanged about his neck, and he were cast into the sea" (Mark 9:42). The Gospel of Matthew records a slightly different version of the proverb that supplies some of the reason why offending children is judged so harshly: "Take heed that ye despise not one of these little ones; for I say unto you, That in heaven their angels do always behold the face of my Father which is in heaven. . . . Even so it is not the will of your Father which is in heaven, that one of these little ones should perish" (Matthew 18:10, 14).

Indeed there are numerous explanations that can be offered to underscore the sanctity of and divine concern shown for little children. But perhaps more important, Jesus showed *his* special concern for them in a dramatic fashion. The proverb recorded by Mark is striking. It says that a person would be better to tie a millstone, which usually weighs several hundred pounds, around their neck and then try to swim in that condition than to offend a little child. In other words, a person would be better off dead than to offend a little child. What is even more striking is that there are no similar statements in the words of the prophets of the Old Testament and therefore Jesus' statement appears more as an exception than a representation of the general outlook of his society.

In the Book of Mormon, children also feature prominently in the words of the prophets, particularly in the teachings of king Benjamin: "And even if it were possible that little children could sin they could not be saved; but I say unto you they are blessed . . . the blood of Christ atoneth for their sins" (Mosiah 3:16). Moreover, Jesus blessed the children of the Nephites before his departure at the end of the first day (3 Nephi 17:21–25).

Jesus showed a particular love for little children in his teachings. On one occasion his disciples felt that they could insulate Jesus from a crowd by sending them away. When it came to Jesus' attention that some little children were being sent away he said, "Suffer little children, and forbid them not, to come unto me: for of such is the kingdom of heaven" (Matthew 19:14). These instances reveal something of Jesus' personal life and concerns, when he was able to teach a principle and at the same time express his great love for children. From his surviving sayings it appears that he was very fond of little children and took notice of them.

Those parables that preserve some hints of Jesus' personal attitudes and emotions show a reflective personality that contemplated rejection by family and friends, the lack of a permanent residence, and that also expressed his concern for children. As a profound teacher, Jesus was also reflective at times, allowing his own concerns to surface in his teachings. His life and experiences influenced the way he taught the gospel. For Jesus, teaching was not simply an academic interest or job that he was required to do.

Proverbs That Teach a Moral Lesson

All teachers have their own unique style in presenting the message and each chooses to address certain topics in his own way. Some teachers prefer to teach through stories that incorporate metaphors and life lessons, while others are more direct and forceful. For example, Nephi in the Book of Mormon had a very distinct style in teaching. He tried to explain his teachings and make everything he taught clear to his audiences. He wanted everyone to understand what he had said ("my soul delighteth in plainness unto my people, that they may learn" 2 Nephi 25:4). Alma, on the other hand, often encouraged his listeners to use introspection and personal reflection in his teachings. He asked numerous challenging questions in his discourses, many of them requiring serious soul searching (Alma 5:16–19). To summarize Nephi's approach we might say that his basic method was to teach truth clearly, which would in turn encourage personal change and conversion. Alma's basic approach was to ask profound questions that would force his listeners to rethink their current presuppositions and ideas. Both approaches are effective.

But how can we really know what characterizes Jesus' teachings in order that we may learn from his particular teaching style? At the beginning of this chapter we considered for a moment how many teachers used proverbs and wise sayings to strengthen their teachings and draw their audiences in. Certainly Jesus did use proverbs frequently. But unlike many who do use this method, Jesus does not appear to have used proverbs to make himself appear wise or to gain credence. Perhaps he used this approach to maintain audience interest or because it was easy to remember the content of his teachings, but unfortunately our sources do not tell us whether this was so. Instead, we have seen that Jesus' proverbs appealed to the ordinary elements of daily life in Galilee, particularly among rural farmers. He seems to have developed a type of working man's or farmer's wisdom that comes through in his sayings. There is no longing for or interest in a life of luxury in his proverbs. Rather, Jesus used working at a plough as a metaphor for living the gospel.

The following proverbs reveal a side of Jesus' personality as well as one of the ways he presented the gospel. He could be direct on occasions—depending on his audience—and at other times he explained his message clearly, but often he would deliver the message in proverbs. These proverbs were easy to remember and have a way of resurfacing in the listener's thoughts days and weeks later. Although he never explicitly stated that he did this purposefully, perhaps this was Jesus' intent. For those who would only hear him once or twice, he taught in a way that would be memorable. In other words, the proverbs of Jesus are often, but not exclusively, aimed at new listeners and followers, particularly those who came to him with questions.

Here are some of the proverbs that he taught that caught the attention of his audiences and disciples. Rather than discuss each of these proverbs individually, they are included here in list form because they have the powerful effect of helping provide a small insight into Jesus and his personality, and particularly into his personal teaching methods.

- "with what measure ye mete, it shall be measured to you" (Mark 4:24). This was a parable common to the Rabbis of a later age. They taught, "The measure with which a man measures on earth, they will measure for him in heaven."[7]
- "For he that hath, to him shall be given: and he that hath not, from him shall be taken even that which he hath" (Mark 4:25).
- "For what shall it profit a man, if he shall gain the whole world, and lose his own soul? Or what shall a man give in exchange for his soul?" (Mark 8:36–37).
- "But I say unto you, That ye resist not evil: but whosoever shall smite thee on the right cheek, turn to him the other also. And if any man will sue thee at the law, and take away thy coat, let him have thy cloke also. And whosoever shall compel thee to go a mile, go with him twain. Give to him that asketh thee, and from him that would borrow of thee turn not thou away" (Matthew 5:39–42).

- "No man can serve two masters: for either he will hate the one, and love the other; or else he will hold to the one, and despise the other. Ye cannot serve God and mammon" (Matthew 6:24).
- "For every one shall be salted with fire, and every sacrifice shall be salted with salt" (Mark 9:49). This proverb quotes Leviticus 2:13.
- "Lay not up for yourselves treasures upon earth, where moth and rust doth corrupt, and where thieves break through and steal: But lay up for yourselves treasures in heaven, where neither moth nor rust doth corrupt, and where thieves do not break through nor steal: For where your treasure is, there will your heart be also" (Matthew 6:19–21).
- "The light of the body is the eye: if therefore thine eye be single, thy whole body shall be full of light. But if thine eye be evil, thy whole body shall be full of darkness. If therefore the light that is in thee be darkness, how great is that darkness" (Matthew 6:22–23).
- "Enter ye in at the strait gate: for wide is the gate, and broad is the way, that leadeth to destruction, and many there be which go in thereat: Because strait is the gate, and narrow is the way, which leadeth unto life, and few there be that find it" (Matthew 7:13–14).
- "Ye shall know them by their fruits. Do men gather grapes of thorns, or figs of thistles? . . . Wherefore by their fruits ye shall know them" (Matthew 7:16, 20).
- "Let them alone: they be blind leaders of the blind. And if the blind lead the blind, both shall fall into the ditch" (Matthew 15:14).
- "Every plant, which my heavenly Father hath not planted, shall be rooted up" (Matthew 15:13).

Almost every one of the above listed parables comes from a single sermon—the Sermon on the Mount. A few of them come from later discourses from the central portion of Jesus' ministry and were delivered to the disciples specifically (those from Matthew 15), but the feature that stands out prominently is that Jesus often used proverbs to teach the gospel to those who were listening to him for the first time or were in the early stages of discipleship.

The proverbs of Jesus also relate eternal truths rather than specific commandments. They speak of the eternities and the general status of mankind. In fact, Jesus rarely spoke of specific commandments in his teachings but rather chose to speak of principles. The proverb form lends itself easily to speaking of principles, but it is much more difficult to compose a proverb that relates a specific commandment.

Another interesting feature of Jesus' teachings is that his mortal brother James—the author of the Epistle of James—also taught using proverbs, but his brother Jude did not, or least none have been preserved in the small epistle attributed to him. The Jewish teachers of Jesus' day were known as *rabbis*, a term that developed fully after Jesus' lifetime, and that in the New Testament does not describe a rabbi as we think of one today. The rabbis in Jesus' time also commonly taught in proverbs, so in this regard Jesus would have been similar to his peers. It would not have seemed out of the ordinary to hear a Jewish teacher using proverbs to present a gospel message. The proverb then is one of the methods of teaching that Jesus had in common with other first-century teachers.

One other truth also seems apparent from a study of Jesus' proverbs: if Jesus chose the teaching moment, then he was more likely to teach in proverbs, but if his opponents chose the setting (or forced the setting), then Jesus was less likely to teach in proverbs. The sheer number of Jesus' proverbs that have been preserved shows that many people thought of him as a great teacher who used wisdom and wit.

SUMMARY

Jesus presented the gospel message by using proverbs or wise sayings. In an oral culture this would have encouraged followers to remember the core principles of what he taught. His use of proverbs also tells us something about the tone of Jesus' message; instead of teaching using the rabbinic methods of quoting previous rabbis, Jesus taught principles that transcended the immediate debates of his age and answered larger cosmic questions.

The proverbs of Jesus also reveal a very personal side of the Savior. They tell us something about where he was from and how he reacted to the government and society of his day. His proverbs do not offer political satire, but instead promote the ideals of the Galilean class of citizens who worked to survive. Some of the proverbs were severe or stern; and those who followed him may have recognized a certain degree of sternness in his character.

All of us have heard a teacher who teaches using such witticisms and proverbial sayings. And while some of these teachers are more satisfying than others, the evidence points to the simple fact that it is one of the chief characteristics of Jesus' teaching style. As we seek to become excellent teachers, it is important to pause and consider what the proverbs were able to convey in Jesus' teachings. We may not necessarily need to emulate the method, but we should strive for the same end result. More than anything, the proverbs conveyed the teacher's impressions of his surroundings while at the same time teaching eternal truths. They were also easy to remember and repeat, thus giving them a timeless quality, particularly for those who were hearing Jesus for the first time.

ATTRIBUTE 3

Maintaining the Spirit While Dealing With Controversy

The opposition to Jesus at a glance:

- Local citizens from Jesus' childhood town attempted to kill him (Luke 4:16–30).

- On at least nine occasions, Jesus was either threatened with death or made plans based on the fact that people were attempting to take his life.

- Jesus physically provoked the Jewish temple authorities on at least two occasions (John 2:13–22; Matthew 21:12–16).

- Jesus asked questions that no one was able to answer (see Matthew 22:41–46).

- Jesus' brothers taunted him and suggested that he put his life in danger to prove himself (John 7:1–9).

- Jesus taught using hyperbole (Matthew 19:24) and pun (Matthew 16:18), which at times appears to have driven people away.

- On occasion Jesus astounded his audiences with what he taught or how he taught (Matthew 7:28; 22:33).

A SOFT ANSWER: HANDLING
OPPOSITION AND CONTROVERSY

One of the most difficult issues a teacher can face in a classroom is an intentionally disruptive comment or open hostility. Instructive momentum flees almost immediately in these situations and continuity comes to an abrupt halt. Gifted teachers are able to control these situations and seasoned teachers are generally able to avoid them. Jesus, like many of the prophets of the Old Testament and a few of the Book of Mormon prophets, faced significant opposition to his teachings. On numerous occasions his teachings and thoughts were challenged. In several instances, the opposition to what he taught became so intense that his life was in danger. In those instances, it would have been so easy for Jesus to use anger or physical force to work his way out of them. Instead, Jesus' method for handling these volatile situations can teach us profound lessons on how to act in similar situations.

Consider for a moment the following details from Jesus' ministry: on at least two occasions, and possibly three, the Jews attempted to stone Jesus[1] (John 8:59; 10:31; 11:8); citizens from his hometown of Nazareth tried to throw him off a cliff (Luke 4:28–32); Jesus was taunted and provoked (Luke 11:53); he was told to hide because Herod Antipas wanted to kill him (Luke 13:31); some Jews openly mocked him (Luke 16:14); a plot developed wherein some leaders conspired to kill him (John 5:16); and the chief priests and Pharisees sent men to arrest Jesus on at least two occasions (John 7:32, 45; 11:57).

In addition to these instances of persecution, many Jews openly challenged Jesus because of his teachings, and many times the Pharisees tried to embarrass him publicly by demonstrating what they thought were contradictions in his teachings. And yet, according to the Gospels, Jesus was never beaten up, physically abused, or even spit upon during his mortal ministry until after the triumphal entry had taken place when his opponents succeeded in arranging his arrest and taking his life.

It is remarkable indeed that an individual who generated so much controversy in his life was possibly able to avoid the physical attacks, at least for a time, that other prophets and apostles have experienced. In fact, Jesus' experience would be in sharp contrast to the Prophet Joseph Smith's and other early Latter-day Saint leaders who suffered tarring and feathering, beatings, and other physical abuses. It is possible that the Gospels authors intentionally avoided any references to these experiences for doctrinal reasons, although there is no surviving evidence to suggest this.

How then was Jesus able to avoid the physical attacks that would naturally have accompanied the controversy he engendered, or did he? Perhaps the most popular answer to this question, and the response that has shaped the way we view Jesus, is the belief that Jesus' powerful presence caused people to respect him. In other words, people respected Jesus because of his physical appearance and strength or the divinity implied in his presence. Even though the image of the lordly and magisterial Jesus is now ingrained into our popular thinking, there is a potential problem with it. The one prophet who may have left us a report of his physical appearance said, "he hath no form nor comeliness: and when we shall see him, there is no beauty that we should desire him" (Isaiah 53:2). Isaiah's prophecy makes him appear very ordinary in appearance rather than magisterial and powerful. Today when we see paintings and other depictions of Jesus, there is usually light emanating from his features. We must keep in mind that these depictions are meant to teach something about Jesus, but those who knew him did not have the benefit of seeing a physical sign that would indicate to them that they were speaking with the Lord. As far as we know, Jesus, looked very mortal and did not stand out physically from his peers. Or at least no one ever noted this about him.

Another answer to this question that has significantly shaped the way we think of Jesus is the one offered in the Gospels. Matthew, Mark, and Luke each carefully crafted the story of Jesus to show that he gave the perfect answers in challenging situations. They wanted to emphasize that Jesus was the perfect teacher, and therefore may have, in certain instances, altered the order of certain events to help them tell the story in the way that they understood it. That is not to say that they falsified their accounts or created stories and put them into Jesus' mouth, but the numerous differences in setting, location, and order of events cannot all be harmonized into a single perfect picture. There can only be one verifiable historical setting and the variations must be attributed to either misinformation, later change to the story, or doctrinal motivation.

The story of Jesus stilling the Sea of Galilee at night is an excellent example of this, and it also shows how each author saw the story in his own way. The first person to record the story in print, at least as far as our knowledge of history permits us to say, was the author of the Gospel of Mark.[2] According to the Gospel of Mark, Jesus was teaching near the

Sea of Galilee and later that same day he entered a boat with his disciples. Also on that day, Jesus delivered four of his most famous parables (the sower, the candle under a bushel, the seed growing secretly, and the mustard seed). After boarding the boat, Jesus decided that he wanted to cross over the Sea of Galilee toward a small city known as Gadara (Mark 4:35; 5:1).

Matthew, probably the second person to record the story, preserved the story almost exactly as Mark reported it, but he chose to alter the setting of the story. In fact, in the Gospel of Matthew the four parables that are delivered just before the stilling of the storm are recorded many months later in Jesus' public ministry (Matthew 13). Instead, according to Matthew's account, Jesus spent the day healing the sick and answering questions about the gospel prior to entering the boat and crossing the Sea of Galilee. Jesus and the disciples also sailed to Gergasa instead of Gadara as in Mark.

Luke, who probably wrote after Matthew and Mark, was now faced with a difficult decision. Would he follow the setting of the story as recorded by Mark or would he follow Matthew's account? Interestingly, he chose to do neither and instead offered a third setting for the story. According to him, Jesus delivered some of the teachings of the Sermon on the Mount before he entered a boat and stilled the storm (Luke 8:16–25). After having taught these truths and performing the spectacular calming of the Sea of Galilee, his mother and brothers came to see him (Luke 8:19–21). Jesus then took the opportunity to teach his audience about fellowship in the kingdom and the family of God, probably drawing on the fact that his own family was present on the occasion. Several days later, according to Luke, Jesus entered into a boat and went with his disciples to a city named Gadara (Luke 8:22).

So, all three authors record the story in a slightly different setting. Did Jesus deliver his famous discourse on parables the day he left? Did he heal the sick the day he left? Or did he redeliver some of his teachings from the Sermon on the Mount and then depart a few days later to Gadara? Perhaps some of the details can be harmonized so that Jesus could have done all of these things prior to leaving. The difficulty with this approach is that the same authors also preserve the stories leading up to the stilling storm as they are recorded in the other Gospels, except they include them in different settings. So now we would have to suppose that Jesus spoke of his mother and brother prior to leaving for Gadara, and then again much later after his return from Gadara (Matthew 12:46–50). In other words, Jesus would have had to deliver many of his sayings on three different occasions and in three different settings to make the stories harmonious.

Another look at the story in its various settings reveals a few powerful truths. First, each of the three authors to record it was careful to preserve the story in nearly identical language although they were willing to alter the setting according to their choosing and based on the information available to them. This would indicate that the words of Jesus were sacred and were not altered significantly, but the order of the story was not yet rigidly established. Second, we learn that Mark tells the story without making any connections to the previous story. Jesus taught in parables and then crossed the Sea of Galilee. There does not appear to be any motive behind the order of the story. It appears that Mark is simply telling the story as he received it. Next, Matthew taught that Jesus performed a series of powerful miracles on a single day, a series of signs. Jesus healed the sick and then someone approached him with a question that showed less than perfect faith. To show how others were similarly wavering in their faith (including the disciples), Matthew presents Jesus' most powerful miracle to date—the stilling of the storm. Finally, Luke places the story in the context of Jesus teaching his followers about not hiding the truth and their testimonies. Immediately after these teachings, Jesus' own family comes to see him, some of whom we learn did not believe in Jesus (John 7:3, 5). Jesus, in a way, could be accused of not letting his light shine for his own family. To remedy any apparent confusion on this matter, Luke then records a very powerful miracle, Jesus' most dramatic miracle to date, which shows that all nature was able to see the light and power of Jesus. Luke thereby removes any questions some might have concerning whether Jesus made his light shine sufficiently to his own family.

Returning back to our previous discussion, this incident, as reported by Luke (and to a lesser extent Matthew), shows Jesus as the perfect teacher. He practiced what he taught. He let his light shine to the world literally right after he said it. But was that the way it really happened? That answer is almost impossible to discover from the sources currently available to us. However, one thing stands out about Jesus: he was able to teach powerful lessons both in word and in deed rather than relying only on his charismatic personality. As Matthew and Luke tell the story, they both raise significant questions prior to relating the story and then show

how the miracle provided a physical answer to those questions. This is certainly an example of teaching by word and deed.

Concerning the issue of how Jesus might have been able to avoid the physical attacks that frequently accompany persecution, we might take our cue from the Gospel authors, who saw in him an amazingly gifted teacher—one who could control setting in order to achieve the greatest results. In other words, he was able to demonstrate as well as teach that what he said was true. Signs accompanied his words. This is at least one reason that Jesus was perhaps able to escape physical abuse. Like Samuel the Lamanite, there was temporary safety and a measure of divine protection in his signs.

Controversies Created by the Sadducees and Pharisees

Before we can look at specific instances of controversy between Jesus and his contemporaries, it will be important to understand the origin of these controversies. Jesus was rarely accused of breaking the commandments of the law of Moses (the accusation that he committed blasphemy was an exception), although on numerous occasions his miracles were interpreted to be contradictory to the law. One major exception to this is that Jesus' opponents regularly claimed he had transgressed the commandment to keep the Sabbath day holy; however, they based this accusation on their interpretation of what it meant to keep the Sabbath day.

In contrast to this, Jesus was frequently accused of breaking the law or of doing things that were not lawful (Matthew 12:1–2). The law in question in these instances was most often the Pharisaic oral law, and sometimes Jesus did do something that seemed to contradict common practice or popular understanding of the law. Because of these frequent accusations, it is apparent that most of his opponents would not have considered Jesus sinless as we do today (John 9:24), and many who knew of him would also have felt some uneasiness with his stance toward the popular oral law. In fact, the Gospels (the only surviving biographies of Jesus' life) do not state that he was sinless.[3] That is not a suggestion that he was not sinless, but it reveals that the particular topic of Jesus' sinlessness was not a focus of the ministry or that Jesus did not address the topic. In other words, they did not feel the need to note this important detail about Jesus, either because it was generally well known among those who believed in Jesus or it was simply assumed by the authors.

Nearly a century and a half before Jesus was born, the Pharisees and Sadducees began a struggle to win control of the people of Israel. They sought control over the government and they sought to win the hearts of the people. In a series of seesaw battles that are now considered epic, the Pharisees emerged as the sect of the masses and the Sadducees became the sect of the elite. The vast majority of Jews living at the time of Jesus were neither Pharisee nor Sadducee, but if asked, the majority of commoners would apparently have supported the Pharisees in their beliefs.[4]

As the battle for the hearts of the people, and in particular for the ear of the ruling Herodian family, continued into the first century AD, small towns and villages also saw their share of debates on religious issues. Although the Pharisees were certainly more popular or accepted, the Sadducees were still a dominant force in politics and among the ruling elite. Therefore, an important part of religious and civic life in the first century was characterized by debates between the Pharisees and Sadducees. Typically, those living near Judea and in the Jewish cities of Galilee would have been at least generally aware of the doctrinal positions of these two sects.

When Jesus began teaching the gospel, he did so in these same small towns and villages that had already experienced debates between Pharisees and Sadducees, or among those who defended their beliefs. Many times it is easy to assume that when the Gospels mention Pharisees asking Jesus a question publicly, they were asking as official representatives of the sanctioned position of all Pharisees. This is not necessarily the case because in many instances Jesus was teaching in rural Galilee where there were no official Pharisee representatives. Instead, local Pharisee sympathizers and followers may simply have been asking him questions concerning how Jesus' own teachings compared with the popularly accepted views of the Pharisees. This may explain why in so many instances the debates simply dissolve, and why it is that in the stories of Jesus' arrest and crucifixion there is only one mention of Pharisee involvement (John 18:3). Jesus faced opposition to his teachings from those who favored Pharisee interpretations, but this opposition may have been more loosely construed than we typically assume.

In fact, in the vast majority of instances, Jesus' teachings would have been similar to those of the Pharisees. Because of a number of doctrinal affinities between Jesus' teachings and those of the Pharisees, many Jews of Jesus' day may have assumed that Jesus was a Pharisee with some divergent viewpoints. Jesus' viewpoints were dramatically opposed to those of the Sadducees, but his teachings were often similar to those of the Pharisees. Just a few examples demonstrate the similarities. Both Jesus and the Pharisees taught a universal resurrection, both relied on continuing revelation for guidance, both advocated the teachings of the prophets of former dispensations, and both believed that the Israelites were God's chosen people and that he would again restore them. These are only a few of the many similarities.

HOSTILITY AND CONFLICT: DIFFERENCES BETWEEN JESUS' TEACHINGS AND POPULAR INTERPRETATIONS

Although space will not permit us to look at every single conflict that Jesus experienced, the following stories will help us to see Jesus' remarkable ability to handle volatile situations. Not long after the Twelve Apostles had served a mission to the cities of Galilee and among the Jews (Matthew 10), Jesus and his disciples reunited in Galilee. While together on a Sabbath day, his disciples "began to pluck the ears of corn, and to eat" (Matthew 12:1). This action so disturbed a group of Pharisees (or local onlookers with Pharisaic leanings) that they approached him on the matter and said, "Behold, thy disciples do that which is not lawful to do upon the sabbath day" (Matthew 12:2).

The actual sin of the disciples according to their accusers was that they had plucked the green heads of wheat or barley and were eating them in the fields. According to the law of Moses, a landowner was directed not to glean his fields after the initial harvest, but instead he was commanded, "And when ye reap the harvest of your land, thou shall not wholly reap the corners of thy field, neither shalt thou gather the gleanings of thy harvest. And thou shalt not glean thy vineyard, neither shalt thou gather every grape of thy vineyard; thou shalt leave them for the poor and stranger" (Leviticus 19:9–10). Therefore, Jesus and his disciples (the poor) were permitted to pluck the wheat and eat it as long as they were gleaning or taking from the corners of the field.

The doctrinal challenge arose out of a concern whether or not gleaning violated the commandment to keep the Sabbath as a day of rest. The Pharisees in this instance appear to have placed greater emphasis on the

Lord's commandment to his people when he said, "Six days may work be done; but in the seventh is the sabbath of rest" (Exodus 31:15). In their minds the action of Jesus' disciples constituted an act of work—harvesting or threshing—whereas Jesus appears to have understood it as an act of God in taking care of the poor and hungry. At this point the situation could have easily escalated into a verbal scolding. Jesus was not obligated to accept their viewpoints and Jesus had done nothing wrong. It all came down to the issue over whether picking the heads of wheat on the Sabbath should be considered work or not. But what was as stake was far greater than a simple discussion of law. This attack and others like it were likely intended to turn people's hearts against Jesus and discredit him. His opponents wanted to show that Jesus did not live the law and that he was a sinner since sinners could not do the miracles that Jesus claimed to do or that others had claimed to see and experience.

The brilliance of Jesus' reaction comes in his reply to their challenge. He offered two parallel examples that justified his actions. First, he pointed out that David, when he was fleeing from Saul, entered the Tabernacle and ate of the "shewbread" (Matthew 12:4). This bread, which is akin to the bread used in the sacrament today, was reserved for the Levites to eat. And David, being the anointed king and from the tribe of Judah (not a priestly tribe), was not permitted to eat it. But he did eat it and he was not condemned for doing so (1 Samuel 21:3–6).

Jesus immediately followed this example with another example. According to the law of Moses, a newborn male had to be circumcised on his eighth day of life, even if his eighth day of life fell on the Sabbath (Leviticus 12:1–3). Therefore, all boys who were born on a Friday were circumcised the following Sabbath. This meant that the priests were required to break the law in order to perform an action that constituted work.

Several points emerge from Jesus' response. First, his answer is in part diversionary. The specific question from the Pharisees was whether his disciples' actions constituted work. Instead, Jesus showed that at times God had blessed his anointed in ways that required the bending of a law, and that some parts of God's plan or law are greater than others. In other words, some requirements of the law are greater than others. His answer also diverts attention away from the immediate issue or concern because it makes the listener think about gray areas of the law. For example, was it permissible for David to eat the sacrament bread? As their minds focused away from their immediate concern the Pharisees' anger toward Jesus lessened.

Second, the original question was likely intended to turn the local villagers against Jesus because the Pharisees thought that they could show that Jesus broke the law—he violated the commandment to keep the Sabbath as a day of rest. But Jesus answered more powerfully. His teaching was that some truths or commandments—in these cases the preservation of David's life (the Lord's anointed) and the concern that young boys participate in the proper ordinances at the proper time—were comparatively more important than others. The Lord permitted his future king to eat the sacrament bread, and the Lord permitted the Levites to break the law so that the sons of the Israelites could keep the commandments, specifically by participating in one of the ordinances of the law—circumcision. Jesus' views would have been tremendously popular with common folk, who could now see that the Pharisees' question seemed to be quibbling over trivial matters, much as we might see them today.

Another challenge that Jesus encountered was the important question whether or not a sinner could heal, or whether a person could sin in the process of healing someone else. This question may seem odd today, but in several instances Jesus' opponents felt that he had broken the law in the process of healing. Two of the most important examples come from a healing that took place in Capernaum shortly after Jesus had delivered the Sermon on the Mount and then later during the healing of the man born blind in the city of Jerusalem.

The first example is fairly straightforward. While in Capernaum a small group of believers came to Jesus carrying a man who was "sick of the palsy" (Matthew 9:2). His condition was debilitating because he was not capable of moving off the bed or coming to Jesus on his own. So others brought him to Jesus, perhaps at the man's request, and they seem to have anticipated that Jesus could heal the man. Matthew then interjects into the story the detail that, "certain of the scribes" were also present (Matthew 9:3). These scribes were almost certainly the local Jewish elders who governed the synagogue or Jewish community in the area.

Jesus said to the man in the presence of these elders, "Son, be of good cheer; thy sins be forgiven thee" (Matthew 9:2). Whether he meant for the elders to hear or not, we no longer know. In Jesus' time, like in the modern kingdom, no mortal had the power to forgive or remit sins. At times a bishop, or other appropriate Church leader, may state that a person has been forgiven in the eyes of the Church, but the bishop cannot forgive a person's sins, no matter how sincere the repentance has been. Two thousand years of perspective has actually obscured the original historical question in this instance because our immediate reaction is that of course Jesus can forgive sins. But the issue was not so clear to the members of his audience in that day, who doubted Jesus and questioned him. They did not have a testimony that Jesus was the Savior; they were still struggling over whether there was any truth in the claims that he made.

In this story, Jesus did something remarkable to settle the dispute. Jesus first asked a rhetorical question, one that diverted their attention away from the issue at hand. He asked, "is [it] easier, to say, Thy sins be forgiven thee; or to say, Arise, and walk?" (Matthew 9:5). Of course, it does not really matter which phrase is easier to say—although, incidentally, the phrase "arise, and walk" has fewer words and is technically easier to say, thus arguing that what Jesus did was more difficult. But the heart of the matter is whether Jesus can forgive sins. His first question, as in the previous example, diverted their attention away from their initial concern.

He could also have easily explained who he was or why he had power to forgive sins, but instead he used the priesthood to demonstrate his divinity. He told the assembled audience that he intended to heal the sick man. If the man arose healed, then Jesus had the power to forgive— the miracle would become proof of that fact—but if the man was not healed at Jesus' command, then his opponents were correct and Jesus was a fraud. To their astonishment, Jesus said to the man, "Arise, take up thy bed, and go unto thine house" (Matthew 9:6). Because the man arose and walked back to his own house unassisted, there was no more discussion about whether Jesus could forgive sins. Unfortunately, miracles have a tendency to produce short-term conversions and so these same concerns would resurface again at a later date. We might note that it was Jesus who presented the test and explained what it would mean if the man arose and walked. He was in control of the meaning and outcome in this situation.

John 9 presents another fascinating look into the way Jesus dealt with controversy and conflict. While in Jerusalem, Jesus encountered a man who had been born blind. Jesus' disciples asked a question based on popular assumptions of their day. They asked Jesus whether the man's blindness was a result of a sin the man's parents had committed (during the pregnancy or prior) or a sin the man had committed (while in the pre-mortal world). Jesus answered in a remarkable way. Instead of choosing one of the options presented to him, he taught, "Neither hath this man sinned, nor his parents: but that the works of God should be made manifest in him" (John 9:3). This man was born blind so that Jesus could heal him and teach a powerful lesson. The story contains its own endorsement of how important it is.

Up to this point in Jesus' ministry, he had performed numerous miracles. Many of them were done in public settings where many people could witness them. From a skeptics' viewpoint, however, there was a significant problem with them. First, as we have already seen, many leading authorities believed that Jesus was a sinner, and second there was no way to prove that Jesus had actually performed the healing. If Jesus told someone to be healed and that person was healed, how could anyone be certain that Jesus had done it? Was the healing a pre-arranged setup, or was the healed person simply faking it to draw a crowd? These questions continue to plague modern miracles.

Another interesting facet of the story is that Jesus rarely healed by laying his hands on someone and commanding the person to be healed. Instead, people touched him (Matthew 9:20–22), he healed from long distances (Matthew 8:5–13), he spit on people (Mark 7:33; Mark 8:23), and he commanded people (John 5:8) to name just a few of the methods he used. And even though Jesus' miracles were numerous, the unbelieving still had some difficulty accepting Jesus' role in those miracles because they thought he was a sinner.

The story of the man born blind offers a powerful solution to this problem because it demonstrates that Jesus did indeed heal the man. Some details in this story are difficult for modern sensibilities to comprehend, but Jesus was trying to show his audience that something from him physically entered into the blind man and healed him. Presumably there could be no doubt that Jesus had healed the man.

In front of everyone assembled, Jesus bent down, spit upon the ground, and made a small amount of clay with the spittle. He then took that clay and put it on the eyes of the blind man whom he also told to go and wash in the Pool of Siloam (John 9:6–7). The man did so and when he returned he could see. Something from Jesus (his spittle) healed the man when it touched him. But herein Jesus created a controversy because his act of making clay was perceived to violate the Sabbath day commandment prohibiting work. Even though the issue of work may seem ridiculously small in this instance, the question was centered on the issue of whether it was work at all. To Jesus' opponents the question was not whether the work resulted in something good or whether it was small, the question was whether it was work by definition.

In the Pharisees' subsequent interrogation of the man who had been healed, they asked him, "What did he to thee? *how opened he thine eyes?*" (John 9:26; emphasis added). They believed or had decided that a person who sinned could not also perform a miracle. The belief is not misguided. The Book of Mormon confirms, "and there was not any man who could do a miracle in the name of Jesus save he were cleansed every whit from his iniquity" (3 Nephi 8:1; emphasis added). Although there is a small difference in the two passages—in the Book of Mormon the person is forgiven, and in the New Testament the issue is continuing to sin—the conclusion in both is that a person needs to be clean to use the priesthood and heal.

In the previous examples we saw that Jesus diffused a volatile situation by diverting his audiences' attention and then used the situation to bear testimony of his ministry. In this instance, Jesus used a volatile situation to allow an interested or intrigued listener to become a strong follower. As John said at the beginning of the story, the man was born blind, "that the works of God should be made manifest in him" (John 9:3). Jesus then allowed that man, after his healing had taken place, to carry the burden of the controversy himself, and to be challenged on some important doctrinal issues. The man's family was also called in and interrogated (John 9:18–22). Finally, in exasperation, the man asked his questioners whether they were challenging him because they wanted to become followers of Jesus (John 9:27). The Pharisees then accused the man of not following God and having been duped by a religious charlatan.

When the man finally found Jesus again, "he said, Lord, I believe. And he worshipped him" (John 9:38). The controversy turned into something important and meaningful for the young man, and even though the hostility toward Jesus continued to grow in power and clarity of purpose, a powerful conversion grew out of it.

Jesus faced numerous other difficult and challenging situations, some of which we will look at later. In all of these, Jesus achieved positive results, whether it was testifying of his mission or strengthening the faith of those who were weak in their faith. In only one instance in the entire New Testament does it say that Jesus reacted in anger. Mark reports that, "And when he had looked round about on them with anger . . . he saith unto the man" (Mark 3:5). Whether this was Mark's assumption of what Jesus was feeling or it was the assumption of the audience who heard Jesus on that day, it still stands out as a unique reaction on Jesus' part. Our sources do not note that he became angry or enraged at the numerous silly questions that were asked of him, even though we might expect such a reaction.

Instead, Jesus reacted by asking challenging questions, diverting his opponents' wrath away from their initial question, testifying of his ministry, and by taking the opportunity to teach powerful truths. In all of the instances where Jesus faced the anger of his opponents, Jesus did not back down. He stood tall against his enemies, with power and poise. They challenged him, but he challenged their beliefs also, and, as the New Testament records, Jesus came off as victor while his opponents only succeeded in taking his life.

Summary

As a masterful teacher, Jesus diffused a number of volatile situations and was able to teach to many despite the hostility of a few. In some instances, he used the hostility to help new followers stand on their own and learn to witness for themselves their faith in Jesus. But we also see that Jesus, in answering his critics, almost always attempted to divert the anger of his opponents. Nearly always his first question or response seems intended to direct his audience's attention toward another subject. Instead of answering the immediate challenge and thus becoming embroiled in a fight of words and personal interpretations, Jesus drew attention toward concepts and principles.

In settings where a teacher is challenged, particularly when that challenge is hostile, it is human nature to seek to answer the problem at hand by responding specifically and with clarity to the question that has been posed. That was not, however, Jesus' method of handling challenging questions and hostility. He maintained his calm, he did not ignore, he did not ridicule, but instead he regained control of the direction of the conversation and then he offered his own viewpoints, usually using the scriptures or stories from the scriptures to build his answer. In those stories where the Gospels record hostile overtones or implications in the questions presented to Jesus, it is instructive to follow the pattern of the great master teacher who was able to turn those questions to his advantage.

ATTRIBUTE 4

$$\infty$$

Teaching by Command
Or by Stories

JESUS' COMMANDMENTS AT A GLANCE:

The Gospels do not attribute many new commandments to Jesus. He did, however, deliver, among others, the following commandments:

- "Come unto me" (Luke 18:16)
- "This is my commandment, That ye love one another, as I have loved you" (John 15:12)
- "I say unto you, That whosoever is angry with his brother without a cause shall be in danger of the judgment" (Matthew 5:22)
- "Whosoever looketh on a woman to lust after her hath committed adultery with her already in his heart" (Matthew 5:28)

The Gospel authors preferred to tell the stories of Jesus' life, wherein he commanded people and things. For example:

- Jesus said, "Peace, be still," thus commanding an entire sea to be calm (Mark 4:39)
- He commanded the dead to rise (Mark 5:22–24, 35–43)
- He cast out a devil (Mark 5:1–19)
- He commanded people to do things in order to be healed (Matthew 12:10–13)

The Narratives and Commands of Jesus

In our modern world, Jesus is often thought of as holding views that were contrary to the Jewish law, as having spoken against the temple, and as having spoken against what Judaism had become in his day. According to this view, Jesus was somehow born into a society that he sought to radically restructure and to which he often offered strong and cutting critiques. This view is often expressed in terms of the higher law, which Jesus brought to all those who would follow him, and the lower law to which the Jews were inextricably tied. By implication, the Jews needed to accept a higher law in order to continue to be God's chosen people. And yet, even as we say this, we realize that for nearly two millennia that same lower law was the Lord's law of salvation for his people. There were no other options until the Lord led away a small group of faithful followers and taught them differently. For the vast majority of the house of Israel, the law of Moses was (and still is today) the divinely inspired word of God.

At the heart of the differences between Jesus and his contemporaries is whether or not he typically rebuked, criticized, challenged, encouraged, or used other ways of pointing out differences. Whatever the differences between Jesus and his countrymen may have been (we will explore them in more depth below), the question arises as to how Jesus treated those differences.

When faced with differences, some tend to push their way through the problem and consider the consequences later. Others see difference as a source of contention, and often express their opposing views in a way that sharpens those differences. And others seek resolution when differences are perceived, hoping to avoid conflict and difficulty. Certainly these three approaches do not describe all of the possible responses to handling controversy, but they are three of the most common. As for Jesus' method of teaching, the question becomes whether he was of one of three types already mentioned, or whether he dealt with challenges in other ways.

As we look into his life we see that controversy surrounded him. Some of his opponents presented their questions in hostile ways, perhaps even hoping to provoke him. The story of Jesus' life holds some clues to how he may have handled the challenges presented to him. One of the first interesting clues comes from a note in the Gospels about the physical presence of Jesus. We may have inadvertently fallen into a way of thinking that causes us to see Jesus as distinctly different from his contemporaries. In art, when Jesus appears in popular depictions, he is typically portrayed as taller than his peers, as wearing a different type of clothing, and in many other ways he is marked as physically different. In artwork these differences are meant to express that Jesus was different; something apart from his contemporaries, and in a way this even shows him as believing in something different than his contemporaries did.

But what if Jesus looked exactly like his peers, perhaps even Jewish in every way. Consider for a moment a detail from a story that may have slipped by unnoticed. According to the Gospels of Matthew, Mark, and Luke, Jesus healed a noble man's daughter. Mark informs us that the man's name was Jairus and that he was a ruler of the synagogue (Mark 5:22). While Jesus was on his way to Jairus' home, a woman, "which had an issue of blood twelve years," came and touched Jesus' clothing (Mark 5:25, 27). We would naturally assume that she came and grabbed Jesus' outer cloak or robe, and that Jesus turned around to see who had touched him.

As part of the law of Moses, Jewish men wore fringes on the border of their clothing to remind them of the 613 commandments that God had given them. Those fringes are specified in Numbers where the Lord said to Moses, "Speak unto the children of Israel, and bid them that they make fringes in the borders of their garments throughout their generations, and that they put upon the fringe of the borders a ribband of blue: And it shall be unto you for a fringe, that ye may look upon it, and remember all the commandments of the Lord, and do them; and that ye seek not after your own heart and your own eyes, after which ye use to go a whoring" (15:38–39). The Lord commanded Moses to have the Israelites add fringes to the hem of their clothes as a memorial and thereby it became a reminder of God's law to his people. Jesus lived the law, but we rarely think of him as an obedient Jew who wore the clothing typical of other Jews in his day, (i.e. wearing fringes on the hem of his garment).

Returning to the story of the woman with an issue of blood, we might ask what part of Jesus' robe she actually touched. We can safely assume that she touched the fringe, the very fringe that the law of Moses directed Jesus and other Jews to wear. The reason that we can assume this is that in the next chapter of the Gospel of Mark, we learn that *Jesus did wear fringes on his robes*: "And whithersoever he entered, into villages, or cities, or country, they laid the sick in the streets, and besought him that they might touch if it were but the *border* (Greek "fringe") of his garment" (Mark 6:56; emphasis added). From this story it is apparent that Jesus dressed like his Jewish contemporaries, as the law directed them to do. At least in one aspect, Jesus looked like his countrymen.

He was like them in wearing the fringes commanded by the law of Moses and perhaps he was like them in other ways also. It would be surprising if Jesus was *against* the law of Moses and its commandments concerning dress and other matters because it was a law he revealed and taught. Some may hold that he was against what that law had become, but perhaps even here we might be able to add nuance to that claim.

So to begin the discussion of Jesus' commandments and how his teachings related to the law of Moses, it is important to see at first that he was very much like his countrymen in many ways. Assuming that he advocated changes, which becomes obvious as we read the Gospels, we can also see that he was a reformer from the inside out rather than someone who sought change from the outside. He advocated seeing the law of Moses in a different light, and therefore his message—that he was the Christ and that he had a higher law that built upon and departed from the Jewish law—would have been an even more radical proposition.

How Jesus Commanded Others

If indeed Jesus brought a higher law that reformed the law of Judaism, then we ought to be able to define that higher law using Jesus' teachings. At the same time, we should study the approach he used in expressing that higher law so that we might also strengthen our own ability to teach new concepts and principles. The differences between what Jesus taught and the law of Moses should give us an indication of the higher law and what it entailed. Surprisingly, however, Jesus rarely spoke of new commandments or new laws. In fact, in the words of Jesus he gave only one new law or commandment: "This is my commandment, That ye love one another, as I have loved you" (John 15:12). Perhaps this single verse epitomizes what the new law of Jesus entailed. We often think of this new commandment in the context of correction; we may think that the Jews hated one another and were cruel (as epitomized in Jesus' parable about the Good Samaritan). Perhaps it comes as no surprise that the law to love one another was not actually new.

This "new commandment" is actually an old commandment found

in Leviticus, when the Lord told his people, "Thou shalt not avenge, nor bear any grudge against the children of thy people, *but thou shalt love thy neighbour as thyself*" (19:18; emphasis added). So to his first-century, Jewish audience, this commandment would not have sounded like the institution of a higher law, but a call to return to an already existing law of the Lord or to emphasize a different portion of that law that had come to be neglected or deemed of lesser importance. At least in this way, Jesus' teachings would not have seemed stern, new, or even different. Rather they would have seemed to reemphasize an existing aspect of the law.

There are several other potentially "new" commandments of Jesus that do change or alter some aspect of the law of Moses. The Sermon on the Mount is typically viewed as the revelation of that higher law. In fact, some have speculated that the Gospel of Matthew was included first in the canon because it contains that higher law, thus giving it precedence over the other gospel accounts. In that sermon, Jesus revealed five higher laws or commandments, which he gave as a direct correction of the law of Moses.

Each of the five laws is delivered in the context of the law of Moses, or a popular interpretation of it. In the first correction, Jesus said, "Ye have heard that it was said by them of old time, Thou shalt not kill; . . . But I say unto you, That whosoever is angry with his brother without a cause shall be in danger of the judgment" (Matthew 5:21–22).[1] We have already seen that the law of Moses did contain certain aspects of the higher law or that it prefigured it in certain ways. But a number of commandments appear to be specifically altered in the teachings of Jesus. The commandment not to kill, for example, can allow for a number of abuses. It only limits behavior or action, and it gives no direction on emotion or attitude. Theoretically one could avoid killing someone but continue to feel hatred toward that person, although even here the law of Moses directs otherwise: the Jews are to love their neighbors (Leviticus 19:18), the strangers or foreigners among them (Leviticus 19:34), and the Lord (Deuteronomy 11:1). So to a first-century listener, would Jesus' teachings have come across as a correction to the law, or a call to repentance and a clarification as to what the law meant?

The second correction is given to the law of adultery or fornication. Jesus said, "Ye have heard that it was said by them of old time, Thou shalt not commit adultery: But I say unto you, That whosoever looketh on a woman to lust after her hath committed adultery with her already in his heart" (Matthew 5:27–28). Again, the law of Moses could allow for abuse of the original commandment because it only puts limitations on a certain behavior, which theoretically would still permit a number of other inappropriate behaviors to exist without punishment. The original law seems to contain a genuine loophole for sins such as harassment, inappropriate flirtation, the viewing of inappropriate images, and other unacceptable behaviors. But that does not mean that the law was intended to permit such things or that the Jews were doing those things. Laws such as this condemn and prohibit specific actions, whereas principles teach us how to curb thoughts, feelings, and emotions.

Today we have a parallel example in the Word of Wisdom (Doctrine and Covenants 89), which forbids certain foods and drinks, but does not specify certain others that are certainly forbidden also. No one today would argue that the silence of the Word of Wisdom on the subject of illegal drugs is a tacit endorsement that those substances are acceptable. Likewise, because the law of Moses did not specify certain actions in the commandment "Thou shalt not commit adultery" does not mean that other behaviors were acceptable. Instead, Jesus called attention to what the law intended and should mean for everyone. In essence, he was closing a loophole by teaching the principle behind that law. Again it appears that Jesus was calling his Jewish audience to repentance, rather than toward a new law. Perhaps we might better express it as a call to live the law with a higher perspective.

Jesus also offered commentary on three other laws in the Sermon on the Mount. These three laws were the popular understanding of entering into a vow or promise (Matthew 5:33; Leviticus 19:12), the popular *lex talionis* or law of retribution—an eye for an eye (Matthew 5:38; Exodus 21:24), and the commandment to love thy neighbors (Matthew 5:43). The fifth correction offers another interesting insight into Jesus' teaching concerning the law of Judaism. In Matthew 5:43 Jesus says, "Ye have heard that it hath been said, Thou shalt love thy neighbour, and hate thine enemy." The first part of the saying is a direct quotation of Leviticus 19:18, but the second part of the verse ("hate thine enemy") is not found anywhere in the Old Testament. In other words, there is no text of this portion of the verse in the scriptures anywhere, indicating that Jesus was probably commenting on a popular interpretation ("ye have heard that it hath been said") rather than on the written law of Moses.

In this final correction or commentary, it appears that Jesus is amending a popular assumption; namely the idea that loving one's neighbors could allow us to still hate our enemies. To remedy such a misguided conclusion, Jesus offered a strong denunciation of the idea and called into question those who taught such things. The problem is that we do not know exactly where anyone "heard" this saying expressed—perhaps popular imagination. Again, as in all of the previous examples, Jesus called on his audience to return to what the law of Moses originally intended. The commandments and principles were not new; they had simply been changed, neglected, or de-emphasized over time. To us these teachings constitute the higher law, but many (not necessarily all) members of his first-century audiences would have understood what Jesus said to mean that they should repent and return to the law of Moses as God intended it to be lived. These sayings were not new in the sense that they changed or reformulated the old law; rather they emphasized different parts of the law that were apparently not emphasized in Jesus' day.

Another vantage point on these five "new" laws comes from the fact that in each of them Jesus says, "Ye have heard" rather than "It is written." With the partial exception of the final law of Matthew 5, all of these laws were written and revealed centuries before the disciples lived. They were part of Israel's history as were the inspired directions on how they were to be lived. But the statement "Ye have heard" suggests that these laws and their accompanying explanations had been interpreted differently or had come to mean something different in Jesus' day. Jesus appears to be challenging what those laws had come to mean rather than what they said, thus making him an advocate of the law rather than advocating for change. Thus, at a later date, when Christians began to separate themselves from their Jewish communities, form their own churches, and hold their own meetings, some may have felt that these later followers were not true followers of Jesus because Jesus had often endorsed the law in his own teachings. This discussion, perhaps unsurprisingly, blossomed at a much later date when Pharisaic converts to Christianity believed that Christians should be Jews prior to becoming true Christians (Acts 15:1–22).

As we look more closely at the teachings of Jesus, there is currently no evidence that he presented his teachings as a hostile alternative to what the Jews commonly thought or taught. Instead, when Jesus corrected he offered his viewpoint with the introduction, "you have heard" rather than "you are wrong" or "your thoughts on the matter are incorrect." Hostility is indeed difficult to detect in his approach. It also seems true that

Jesus did not browbeat or bully people into thinking his way. Instead, his teaching style seems to be that of reasoning, thinking out the issues, and carefully and patiently presenting his thoughts. Although he did command, his commands were well reasoned and extended with gentleness, not with a harsh voice or with bullying.

In a way, we might call his approach an attempt to build and reform, rather than to tear down and criticize. Our own teaching will benefit greatly as we adopt this approach to building up the kingdom and not trying to dismantle what we perceive to be problems. Jesus certainly offered corrections, but as we see from the above examples, these corrections followed the teachings of the prophets who had lived before him.

OTHER COMMANDS OR COMMANDMENTS THAT JESUS GAVE

Jesus often commanded individuals to do certain things, but typically those commandments came as part of a miracle or healing. For example, Jesus commanded the Sea of Galilee to be calm (Mark 4:36–40; Matthew 8:23–26; Luke 8:22–25); he told the dead to arise (Mark 5:22–24, 35–43; Matthew 9:18–19, 23–26; Luke 8:41–42, 49–56); he told devils to depart (Mark 5:1–19; Matthew 8:28–34; Luke 8:26–39); and he told people to be healed (Mark 3:1–3, 5; Matthew 12:9–10, 13; Luke 6:6–8, 10; Mark 7:32–36). In all of these examples, it is Jesus' voice that commands. On other occasions Jesus commanded people to follow him (Mark 1:16–18; Matthew 4:18–20); he commanded his disciples to go certain places (Matthew 28:10); and he told an arresting party to let his disciples go free (John 18:8). He also commanded in other instances, but he rarely said that his words or teachings were a new commandment.

Looking back on the story of Jesus, we see that he frequently commanded people to do certain things, which would indicate that there was also a commanding side of his personality. Earlier we saw that Jesus presented the differences between his teachings and those of his contemporaries with gentleness and reason. But in looking more broadly into his life we learn that he also had the ability and personality to command when necessary. We might consider this a reasoned but firm approach.

In light of his humble personality, it is perhaps unsurprising that he did not command in his own name, but he frequently commanded individuals without citing any name. In fact, the Gospels writers did not

PREGHIERA DAVANTI AL CROCIFISSO

O alto e glorioso Dio,
illumina el core mio.
Dame fede diricta,
speranza certa,
carità perfecta,
humiltà profonda,
senno e cognoscemento
che io servi li toi comandamenti.

Amen.

Basilica dei Frari - Venezia
Cristo morto,
Transetto braccio destro, (sec. XII), bassorilievo

s 3

remember him asking whether people *could* or *would* do certain things, but rather they remembered that he commanded people to do his will. The Gospel authors remembered Jesus as having a commanding presence that needed little explanation or clarification.

Jesus' preference for and ability to command probably had a powerful mental affect on his followers. First, when he commanded people to be healed, and they were healed, his word itself became powerful. The actual words that he spoke had power in them. The Gospel authors even preserved some of his words in Aramaic rather than translate them because they were so powerful (see Mark 5:41). Second, besides the power of his word, it also gave Jesus a commanding presence among his peers. We have all known people who order other people around. We typically do not maintain a very high opinion of such people in our modern society, unless we respect or revere their words. For example, the Prophet can command and direct us to do things, and we accept it willingly, but we rarely like our bosses to command us. Jesus commanded people in some instances. And some people accepted him as a prophet and even Savior, but other people likely thought of him as presumptuous and bossy. This may explain, in part, the antagonism that his mortal brothers felt toward him (John 7:3, 5).

But did anyone besides a handful of disciples think of him as bringing a new commandment or law and subsequently commanding people to obey that commandment? The answer to this question is: probably not! They knew that he commanded people to do things and that his words had power; they even knew that he differed from some Jewish leaders in his interpretation of the law. But the Gospel authors recorded very few commandments Jesus gave, and in those examples each commandment appears to have its origins in the law of Moses.

Leaving the Disciples to Find Their Way

In many ways, as students of the New Testament, and for clarity in explaining our own religious foundation, we would prefer that Jesus had sat down with his disciples and followers and explained exactly how the Christian church would emerge from its Jewish foundation—how it would be different as well as how it would remain the same. Clarity on this issue even seems essential to many, because a lack of clarity might indicate that Jesus never intended to break away from Judaism. But instead of framing the question in that way, we can look at the issue from the perspective of teaching.

The young apostles had been with Jesus for only three years when he died and left them to lead the fledgling church. As far as training programs go, that is a very short time for such a very heavy responsibility. In that short, three-year period they had to become special witnesses of Christ, they had to learn to receive personal revelation, and they had to learn the doctrine of the kingdom. But as every student knows, when a teacher spells out every single detail of a subject, the student loses the privileges of discovery, finding out on his own, and learning through trial and error.

Mastery of a subject does not imply having learned it entirely from another person, but rather it implies long hours of pondering, searching, seeking, and finding. Jesus appears to have used this message with his disciples when he gave them the opportunity to discover the essential message of his ministry and what that would imply for their Jewish heritage and religion. A couple of brief examples will show that the apostles had the opportunity to learn for themselves, and perhaps make mistakes. We should not fault the apostles for their missteps, nor Jesus for providing only the amount of information he saw fit to give, but rather we should see in their actions a profound teaching method at work. Jesus gave his disciples a chance to both hear the word and then to implement it following the spirit of revelation.

After Jesus' death the disciples did something that helps us see how they understood the direction they were to pursue. For some reasons that are now clear and for others that are still unclear, after the death of Jesus there was confusion over whether Christians should break from the local synagogues, or whether they would reform Judaism according to Christ's teachings. In other words, early Christians sought to understand whether they should leave the synagogues and temple entirely or whether they should stay with them and seek change from the inside out as Jesus had done. Historically, it was nearly a decade later that the name Christians was finally used to describe them as a group separate from Judaism (Acts 11:26), and prior to that they were called the way—that is the other way to be Jewish (Acts 9:2). This is, at least, the way the New Testament texts describe the transition from Judaism to Christianity.

It is possible that Christians did not actually decide to leave the synagogues where they originally worshipped, but rather they were expelled

and excommunicated from their ancestral religion by their Jewish countrymen (John 9:22). Christians may have chosen to continue to worship
in those very synagogues if it were not for local Jews, who believed that
confessing that Jesus was the Christ was blasphemous. Initially it appears
that the Jews pushed Christians onto their own two feet and helped them
find their footing rather than Christians separating themselves because
they had a new law. According to the Gospel of John, this was already
beginning to take place during the mortal ministry. Early Christians' hesitance to leave the synagogues that they were once part of may be a result
of the fact that Jesus attended synagogue (with his disciples) during his
mortal ministry (Luke 4:16). He probably also kept kosher and dressed
like other Jews of his day (see earlier discussion and Acts 10:14).[2] And
given that Jesus' teachings sought for change from within, it appears that
at least initially many believed Jesus only sought to bring Judaism into
line with the spirit of the law of Moses.

Several other surviving details from the period following Jesus' death
show how closely the early church remained tied to its Jewish beginnings:
early Christian leaders went to and participated in temple services (according to the book of Acts, Peter and John went to the temple, *at the hour of
prayer, being the ninth hour*" [Acts 3:1; emphasis added]); they kept kosher
(Acts 10:14); many of them remained in Jerusalem; and many Jews felt that
Christianity was a Jewish heresy rather than a distinct religion of its own.

Luke, the author of Acts, astutely preserves the dual nature of early
worship services when he wrote that the apostles were gathered at the
temple, "daily with one accord . . . *and* breaking bread from house to
house" (Acts 2:46; emphasis added). Apparently they still worshipped
in the Jewish temple and also partook of the sacrament at other members' homes. They continued to follow the teachings of Jesus where he
had given specific instructions, such as regarding the sacrament or Lord's
Supper, and they also continued to follow the teachings of the law of
Moses because Jesus had also lived that law.

One example helps us see how difficult it was for the early Christians
to sever all ties with Judaism and to see Jesus as separate from Judaism.
For many it did not seem correct to completely shun the law of Moses, and
whether out of tradition or habit, many Jews were reluctant to give up such
things as the kosher requirements, the law of animal sacrifice, and other
important practices. Besides Peter, Paul was the most vocal advocate for the
Gentiles in the early Church, and yet Paul was also an example of following

Christ while still maintaining certain practices from the law of Moses.

At the end of Paul's first mission to Cyprus, he faced several significant setbacks because some local leaders in Antioch worried that Paul's mission to the Gentiles would bring people into the fold who did not keep kosher and who were not circumcised, both of which were requirements for Gentiles who wanted to become Jews. Those early leaders, who considered themselves Christians, met to decide whether Gentile Christians needed to keep kosher and be circumcised in order to be accepted into the church (Acts 15:1, 20). And yet nowhere in the New Testament is it recorded that the Lord said that Christians should keep kosher or be circumcised. It was an unspoken assumption. The early Church resolved this issue by convening a general conference.

In all of these examples, we find that some early Christians struggled to break from Judaism. They found some cultural practices and traditions too difficult to give up, and they attempted to make everyone live the law of Moses, even after the Lord had been resurrected. Fortunately, Peter was inspired to redirect some of these misguided practices (Acts 10:9–36; 15:7–11). But behind this is the question of whether they understood Jesus to have given a new or different law apart from the law of Moses.

The answer is obvious that many did not.[3] They thought that Jesus corrected misguided interpretations or popular assumptions, but even some of his followers seem to have thought that he was a reformer of Judaism rather than the messenger of a new religion. These points raise another very important question: "What did Jesus command his followers to do, and which of his teachings embody the higher law?" One of the most difficult things about understanding Jesus' mission from a modern perspective has been the idea that Jesus had to be unique in order to be our Savior. However, it is not necessary that Jesus be unique in order to be profound.[4] In fact, with our eternal perspective on the gospel, we should expect that he would hardly be unique in his teachings, but rather his teachings should align with those teachings he had revealed in his premortal ministry to his people, the Jews.

Thus far we have seen that Jesus was gentle in pointing out differences between his own teachings and the teachings of others, but we have also seen that he could and did command. From the evidence it seems that he was humble but firm, gentle but assertive. The mixing of the two is not easy, and yet it is one of the fundamental characteristics of Jesus' personality as well as his ability to teach the gospel in profound and meaningful ways.

The Heart of Jesus' Teachings and Commandments

There are three things that characterize Jesus' teachings, and hence the law or higher law that he taught. First, he taught that principles are greater than laws and that a person who is living a law can sometimes overlook the principle upon which it is based. Second, he taught that love should direct our actions and decisions. And third, he commanded people to be like him. These three points are the heart and core of the higher law. There is a natural tendency among mankind to prefer physical laws to spiritual principles. The former are easier to monitor, observe, and demonstrate to others. Consider how difficult it would be if a bishop asked, "Do you love one another?" We might say yes, but it would be difficult to prove or demonstrate in any way. It is much easier to have physical evidence for our righteousness.

Returning to the Sermon on the Mount where Jesus delivered his commentary and thoughts upon the law, we see the embodiment of the first principle listed above. Jesus took five commandments or teachings from the law of Moses—the laws of murder and adultery, the popular impressions of how to enter into contracts or oaths, the principle of an eye for an eye, and loving our neighbors—and he reformed them in a spectacular way. Interestingly, Jesus never updated or reformed the laws of tithing, animal sacrifice, the purpose of the temple, or other important teachings and doctrines that have been reformed subsequently, either in the ensuing years after his death or in the Restoration of the gospel. But, he did teach us *how* to reform commandments, and he taught us how to live the principles upon which the laws are based.

When the Lord directed his people to commit no murder, he did not at the same time encourage his people to hate, vilify, persecute, and brutalize others. The law commanded or curtailed an action, but at the same time it permitted certain excesses. It is ridiculous to believe that the law intentionally prohibited a person from taking another's life and at the same time permitted that person to be a persecutor, bully, or aggressor. Although, in a way, the attitude of hatred could persist even though the law controlled the final outcomes of that attitude.

Whether the Jews were actually so mean spirited is a matter of impression today, but it is likely that some excused poor behavior while living the letter of the law. Many others, probably the majority, did not. But certain apparent loopholes made it possible for a person to live the law but not abide by its underlying precept or principle. Jesus corrected this misguided attitude when he taught, "But I say unto you, That whosoever is angry with his brother without a cause shall be in danger of the judgment: and whosoever shall say to his brother, Raca, shall be in danger of the council: but whosoever shall say, Thou fool, shall be in danger of hell fire" (Matthew 5:22–23). The underlying principle had always been that we should love one another and not hate or call one another fools. That the specific principle was not stated during the original revelation does not make it okay to act in anger. Following the teachings of Jesus, the question then becomes, can a person kill someone if they are never angry or if they never think of others as fools?

On another occasion, Jesus taught the principle behind the law of forgiveness. He taught that we should forgive, "Until seventy times seven," in other words indefinitely, even though the wording suggests that after 490 times, one is justified in not forgiving (Matthew 18:22). On other occasions he taught the principles underlying other laws or commandments. For example, he taught that we should not look upon members of the opposite sex with inappropriate thoughts (Matthew 5:28). He taught that we may be asked to sacrifice or give up that which is most difficult for us to offer (Matthew 19:21) and that we should return to heaven having earned interest on the Lord's money (Matthew 25:14–30). He taught about the value of life—"Greater love hath no man than this, that a man lay down his life for his friends" (John 15:13)—and that God loves all his creations (Matthew 6:25–34). This list could be extended considerably, but perhaps more important, we learn that Jesus taught principles. The commandments were already in place (many of them forming part of the law of Moses), and the higher law clarified how we should live those laws to their fullest. Interestingly, Jesus' commanding presence directed us to live the principles. He approached teaching in a way that was familiar to his audiences, but those teachings directed men and women to live in a way that would help them improve their relationship with God and find the greatest rewards in their obedience. We might consider this a way of living the law with a higher perspective.

One of the most profound contrasts of Jesus' ministry was his ability to command the earth, the seas, men, women, and spirits to obey him. They each followed his very word, and in many instances people were healed because they hearkened to those words. Yet even with that commanding and powerful presence, he taught principles and precepts rather than commanding people or ordering them. Herein lies the humility of Jesus. He could easily have commanded men and women to do certain things or to live their lives in certain ways. However, he left agency intact and taught the path to salvation. He had the greatest power to command, and yet he gave few commandments in his mortal ministry.

SUMMARY

Part of human nature is to believe that more of something is better. There are times when it is obvious that less is better, but regarding the commandments of God, there is a tendency to consider that more precise, exact, or carefully considered obedience is greater than simple obedience. Therefore, being more obedient often translates into concerns over what portion of the law we have missed, what areas we might rightly *emphasize* in our obedience, or how we can increase the frequency with which we do things. This process of refining our obedience can yield powerful results, particularly when we recognize important areas that we have previously overlooked. But this practice has a downside also because it can lead to issues of hyper-obedience, or a "higher law" mentality.

When any two people live a similar set of laws, and one of them is obedient to a greater number of laws than the other, there is a natural human tendency to make a comparison, particularly when the two different sets of laws are actually mandated. For example, if two people in the same religion are required to live two separate but related laws, there will be a natural tendency to consider that one person lives the higher law and the other lives the lower law. The conclusion is almost unavoidable because we naturally make comparisons to others when we evaluate our own lives. But a serious flaw exists in this kind of comparison. We must ask ourselves: does God look at me and how I relate to others? In other words, does God judge us by how good or bad those around us are? Is it really true that as long as we are better than those around us, we are doing well? It sometimes seems that way.

Jesus' teachings, and particularly the things that he commanded us to do, provide some powerful answers to these difficult questions. Jesus gave very few new commandments or directives. Perhaps his most powerful directive was the simple statement, "Come unto me" (Luke 18:16; John 6:65), but he rarely said how that was to be accomplished. He never defined exactly what he meant with that directive and others, but relied on us to trust him that he would guide us to salvation. In fact, one of the greatest summaries of Jesus' teachings can be expressed in the simple truth that less is more. He commanded us to love one another, to come unto him, to pray, and to live our lives as he did, but he did not clarify many of the details, which our humanity yearns to find answers to. We seek clarifications on details of the Word of Wisdom, on keeping the Sabbath day holy, and on the proper practice of paying tithing.

Jesus taught us to rely on him, rather than on a set of commandments, for salvation. That is not to say that the commandments are not an important part of salvation (even Jesus made a point of teaching the principles behind some of the commandments), but given human experience, if the commandments were extensive enough to reveal the exact path to salvation, we would focus more on them and consequently Jesus himself would take a back seat role in our salvation. Like the Jewish audiences to whom he taught the gospel, we would focus our attention on the law and live every detail of it with extreme precision. Great good would come of it in many ways, but at the same time, the Lord of salvation then becomes an administrator of the commandments rather than a minister of personal salvation. It seems that Jesus would have been more widely accepted had he spent his time extensively commenting upon the commandments and how his peers had been abusing them. Other popular teachers of his day did that very thing. Instead, he made himself part of the message. The great obstacle that people faced was not their desire *to disobey*, but rather their concern that Jesus preached himself instead of preaching commandments.

There is very little concern expressed in the New Testament that Jesus' commandments were too stringent. The few examples come from a very obedient, young, rich man and one of Jesus' disciples (Matthew 19:16–26). Jesus' commandments were not too difficult to obey, in fact they seem to be in all aspects simpler than the law they had been living. But that is exactly the problem: there were too few new commandments and too much emphasis was placed on Jesus. Many were able to accept this, but many others rejected him because of that very emphasis.

In summary, as we try to shape our own teaching style to reflect the master teacher, we would benefit in many instances from teaching the principles of the gospel rather than focusing on interesting details or areas of peripheral interest.

ATTRIBUTE 5

Using Scripture To Teach

JESUS' USE OF SCRIPTURE AT A GLANCE:

- Jesus quoted the book of Psalms more than any other single book of scripture.
- Isaiah is quoted almost as frequently as the Psalms in the New Testament.
- Psalm 53, which describes the Savior's ministry vividly, is not quoted in the New Testament Gospels.
- The Gospel authors were aware of the fact that Jesus quoted from Psalm 22, the Psalm that speaks of his crucifixion, during the last week of his life.
- Jesus used scripture (Deuteronomy) to rebuff Satan during the temptations.

HOW JESUS INTERPRETED AND USED SCRIPTURE IN HIS TEACHINGS

One of the greatest challenges any organized religion faces or has faced is the question of who has the authority to interpret their sacred texts—the scriptures. Answers to this question range from prophets and apostles, to laymen and scholars. Each religion has responded to the question in a variety of different ways. In the modern era, it is increasingly common to believe that the most eloquent and insightful interpreters have the proper authority. This typically and quickly evolves into scholars becoming the most authoritative source for scripture interpretation, a scenario that was also common in Jesus' day.

Another similar problem is the issue of how to interpret scripture. Responses to this question range from symbolic and allegorical interpretations to historical and literal ones. The person who is commenting on scripture will almost always determine how scripture is read. So, for example, some of us may argue for the historical and literal meaning of scripture where the original setting determines how it is understood, while others will draw upon symbolism to a greater degree. Personality often determines whether others will accept a unique view on scriptures, and this feeds into the modern appetite for being entertained while being taught. Fortunately, the Restoration of the gospel has provided powerful answers to the questions of who can interpret scripture and how we should interpret scripture. We have learned that a prophet is the Lord's mouthpiece, and that other ordained representatives of the Lord carefully follow a divine pattern when interpreting scripture or providing us with new revelation.

But answers to these questions were not so clear in the first century, just as they are not so clear today for the vast majority of Christians. Jews living in the first century might rightly have asked where Jesus received his authority to interpret scripture. They wondered whether he had been schooled (was he a scholar?), or whether he was a Pharisee (a religious authority) in outlook and belief. Some thought his interpretations were self-aggrandizing, and others were confused at how he interpreted scripture.

To help us see how Jesus responded to these challenges in his day—the questions of authority and method—we must try and differentiate Jesus' particular approaches to these questions and then consider examples where he put those methods into practice. To begin with, we must recognize that Jesus was both unique and ordinary in his interpretation of the scriptures of Israel. Some of his interpretations were considered unique because certain important doctrinal truths had been lost over time, yet some of his scriptural teachings were considered ordinary because so many others before him had taught the same things.

It will not be possible to look at every instance in which Jesus commented upon a passage from the Old Testament. The LDS bible dictionary (s.v. "Quotations") contains an extensive list of scriptural parallels and quotations contained in Jesus' teachings. The list is by no means comprehensive, but it offers a fairly wide picture of how he used them. By looking at a few instances in which Jesus relied on the Old Testament to draw out an example, we can learn how he described and characterized his own mission as well as how he interpreted one of the primary sources from which he drew his authority. At the same time, we will see how Jesus used the scriptures to bring power to his teachings, which in turn may help us empower our own teachings by including the scriptures in our lessons.

Jesus' Use of Scripture to Teach His Message

Perhaps it is not surprising that the scriptures contained in the Old Testament preserve very few traces of the doctrine of Christ and Jesus' role as Savior and Redeemer, although there are certainly scattered remnants in the Old Testament. Some notable exceptions are Isaiah 53–54; Psalm 22, and Deuteronomy 18:15–18. For the most part, however, the Old Testament is relatively silent on issues such as Jesus' birth, life, teachings, death, parents, Resurrection, and Messiahship. Some traces are preserved, but the fact that the Book of Mormon is so clear on these same issues leads to the conclusion that the Book of Mormon peoples had a more complete account of Jesus' ministry through either the Plates of Brass, which they brought with them, or through the restoration of these truths by their own prophets.

In Jesus' day there were many alternate voices declaring what the scriptures meant. This included a well-developed tradition of knowledge being passed on through the Rabbis (a scholarly tradition). In fact, the Jews were so careful in their scholarship that they would create genealogies of interpretation. They would say that rabbi so-and-so taught the following, and he was followed by rabbi so-and-so, and so forth. This tradition was already powerfully developed in Jesus' day and it offered a strong counter to Jesus' own interpretation of the scriptures. Jesus did not quote others in his interpretation of scripture; instead he relied on his own authority from the Father. This approach caused some people to view Jesus as self-promoting and probably also egocentric (Matthew 7:28–29).[1] They may have even pressed him to be more scholarly in his conclusions and to rely less on the intangibles of feeling and emotion.

Consider the following story from Nazareth, Jesus' boyhood town where many of the locals knew him and his family. At the very beginning of his public ministry, Jesus entered the local synagogue or gathering place in Nazareth, probably because he wanted to pray and ponder the scriptures. According to Luke, he did not initiate the discussion, but rather he had intended to participate as others would have done. On that special Saturday (the Jewish Sabbath), the local congregation gathered to discuss Isaiah 61:1–2, a passage that is now viewed as prophetic of Jesus' ministry, and probably in his day was seen as prophetic of the Messiah. When he went into the synagogue that day, Jesus offered to read the passage of scripture (Luke 4:16–19). According to Jewish custom, Jesus would have stood in place when he read. Perhaps he wanted to read the scripture because it spoke of his upcoming ministry, or perhaps he simply wanted to participate in the discussion.

After he read the passage, some of those in attendance wanted Jesus to offer some type of commentary on the passage. Whether he had originally intended to do so is now unknown, but at least some in the crowd expected him to say something about the passage he had read. According to Luke, Jesus sat down (Luke 4:20), thus likely indicating that he did not originally intend to comment on the passage, even though it clearly defined his teaching ministry. But the events that follow reveal something of how his neighbors and friends saw him. Perhaps they knew he considered himself to be the Messiah; perhaps they were excited to hear someone proclaim that they were living in the "acceptable year of the Lord;" or perhaps Jesus was simply a powerful teacher. In any case, they waited for him to make a comment, and when he sat down, "the eyes of all of them that were in the synagogue were fastened on him" (Luke 4:20). They looked to him for further instruction, something that demonstrates that the message initially started off on the right foot.

Jesus stood, according to their desires, and offered a simple commentary on this passage: "This day is this scripture fulfilled in your ears" (Luke 4:21). This saying can mean a variety of different things; the Greek translation of what Jesus said offers no clear interpretation of what he meant. He could have meant that they were living in the day when that particular scripture would be fulfilled; he could have meant that the scripture was being fulfilled among them because they were the poor who were hearing the gospel. Or he could have meant that he was the literal fulfillment of the Isaiah passage.

In other words, he could have meant that Isaiah was speaking of Jesus of Nazareth when Isaiah said, "The Spirit of the Lord God is upon me; because the Lord hath anointed me to preach good tidings unto the meek; he hath sent me to bind up the brokenhearted, to proclaim liberty to the captives, and the opening of the prison to them that are bound; To proclaim the acceptable year of the Lord, and the day of vengeance of our God; to comfort all that mourn" (Isaiah 61:1–2). Today, we would be inclined to interpret the passage as though Jesus was referring to himself because we understand the overtones of the Isaiah passage, but we cannot be certain of Jesus' intent in saying, "This day is this scripture fulfilled in your ears."

It is telling that the audience in Nazareth assumed that Jesus meant he was the literal fulfillment of Isaiah 61:1–2. Because of their negative view of what Jesus had said, they challenged him on an important point. Popular understanding of the Messiah taught them that the Messiah would be a royal figure, a prophet, agent of God, or representative of the Davidic line. A peasant or local Messiah was problematic to them because they thought they knew who Jesus' mortal father was (meaning he could not fulfill the prophecies as they understood them) and that he should have been immortal or divinely anointed, rather than a local Jewish artisan from Nazareth. Their popular interpretations of scripture confused them when they were faced with a divine interpretation of scripture.

This Isaiah passage provided Jesus an opportunity to discuss and teach a more accurate understanding of who the Messiah would be. Jesus did not explicitly teach that he was that Messiah on that day, although the faithful could have seen that his intention may have been to convey that idea. Rather, he drew upon the words of the prophets to correct them and to point to his own ministry. One thing that we may be able to learn from this example is that when Jesus was confronted with a passage of scripture that spoke prophetically of his own ministry, he alluded to the fact that he fulfilled it, but he did not explicitly declare himself. There was enough clarity for Jesus' followers to hear the testimony of his words, but there was enough ambiguity in his words that the general audience would not lynch him for his words. Had he specifically declared his Messiahship, there may have been those in the audience who would have used that against him in building a case of blasphemy.

Remarkably, at a later point, Jesus did not apply to himself the most famous passages from the Old Testament that testified of his mission, thus following the same careful approach that he had used earlier in the disputation at Nazareth. Some passages from the Old Testament speak plainly of the Messiah: "For he shall grow up before him as a tender plant. . . . He is despised and rejected of men. . . . Surely he hath borne our griefs. . . . But he was wounded for our transgressions" (Isaiah 53:2–5). Other passages speak of the Savior with equal clarity, but Jesus either did not use them to testify of his own ministry, or those who wrote about him did not remember that he did so. Jesus seems to have been more cautious in his approach, avoiding clear and precise declarations in preference to suggestive references and comments. Later that would change, when Jesus declared his ministry openly, but the early part of his ministry is characterized by a more cautious and careful use of the scriptures.

Instead of using the scriptures to testify openly, Jesus used them as a powerful teaching tool to counter popular misconceptions and assumptions. He focused on scriptures that were part of the popular public discussion about the Messiah. He could easily have sat down with his followers and even antagonists and taught them concerning his own mission, how prophets had foretold his life and death, and the necessity of a Savior, but for reasons now unknown to us, he chose not to. One reason for this, as mentioned above, may be that he needed time to organize the kingdom and call disciples before his death. Had he taught certain truths with absolute clarity early on, the opposition to him may have grown to quickly.

One of the first lessons that we can draw from Jesus' use of scripture in his teachings is a profound resistance to draw upon those passages that spoke most clearly of his ministry. Perhaps this was an issue of humility; the Gospels authors remained silent on why the Lord did not specifically detail the events of his mortal ministry using the scriptures of the Old Testament. What they did note is that Jesus often reflected upon the meaning of the scriptures in his own life and used them to establish certain truths contrary to the popular assumptions of his contemporaries. Like his peers, however, he was intimately aware of the contents of the Old Testament and alluded to the writings of Moses, the Psalms, and the prophets on numerous occasions.

Using the Scriptures to Challenge Assumptions

One of the great challenges for Jews of Jesus' day was the issue of where Jesus was born. In our day, we have an account of Jesus' birth in Bethlehem, which fulfills the prophecy of Micah (5:2). We also have a prophecy in the Book of Mormon concerning Jesus' birth (1 Nephi 11:13–21), which adds clarity to some of the details concerning his birth. But Jesus' audiences did not appear to know the simple fact that he was actually born in Bethlehem, even though he was raised in Nazareth. On numerous occasions, he was challenged concerning his birthplace. Some mocked him in Jerusalem, remarking, "Shall Christ come out of Galilee?" (John 7:41). Later, Nicodemus was reprimanded by some of his own countrymen: "Search, and look: for out of Galilee ariseth no prophet" (John 7:52). It would have been so easy for Jesus to clarify this conclusion by citing the appropriate scriptures and then testifying of his true birthplace. Instead, the Jews allowed their scriptural interpretation to impede them from coming unto Christ.

Other popular assumptions also hampered people from fully accepting Jesus as the Lord's anointed. One that seemed to offer significant confusion was the belief that the Messiah would be of the lineage of David, and therefore of the tribe of Judah. The Messiah's lineage from David would enable him to rule Israel as David had (2 Samuel 7:16; Isaiah 11:1–5; Jeremiah 23:5–6). The prophecies seem so obvious to understand, and yet Jesus' lineage appeared to contradict the claim that he was the Messiah because they knew him as a man from Nazareth in Galilee. According to his detractors, Jesus was not from the city of David (Bethlehem), he was not of Davidic descent (Judah), and he was not of royal lineage. Again, it would have been easy for Jesus to present them with his genealogy as Matthew (1:1–16) or Luke (3:23–38) presented it. Both genealogies trace Jesus' lineage back to David, and producing this information would have at least settled some concerns.

Instead, Jesus chose to draw on other scriptures, sometimes the very ones that seem to have caused the confusion in the first place, to challenge these common assumptions. In one of the few questions that Jesus asked of the Pharisees, he said, "What think ye of Christ [the Messiah]? whose son is he?" (Matthew 22:42).[2] The question appears very straightforward and the obvious answer is that the Messiah will be "The Son of David." But the answer was also a logical trap because it challenged a common assumption that was impeding some Jews from coming unto Christ. Jesus then asked, "How then doth David in spirit call him Lord, saying, The Lord said unto my Lord, Sit thou on my right hand, till I make thine enemies thy footstool?

If David then call him Lord, how is he his son?" (Matthew 22:42–44). The Savior here quoted from Psalm 110:1 to demonstrate his point.

Expressed more simply, Jesus asked them how the Messiah could be both the son of David and also David's Lord. The answer may seem obvious today because we understand the doctrine of the premortal existence when Jesus was David's Lord. But Jesus' listeners did not understand how these doctrines related. The question further confused them because the doctrine of premortality is not plain in the Old Testament, although some references to it do survive (Jeremiah 1:5). In fact, Matthew notes dryly that the Pharisees were confounded by this question, "And no man was able to answer him a word, neither durst any man from that day forth ask him any more questions" (Matthew 22:46).

They were struggling over whether Jesus could be the Messiah because they thought they knew his father and where he was born. From their perspective, these facts did not match the prophecies relating to the Messiah. Sadly, in the end, what they supposed to be true was what genuinely confused them. Jesus used the scriptures to teach the Jews that they did not know everything about the Messiah, particularly the Messiah's relationship to David. His intent seems to have been to raise questions and to challenge their misguided assumptions, which would in turn cause them to question more broadly in the hopes that some of them would be able to understand that Jesus of Nazareth was also Jesus the Christ. Again, popular interpretation of the scriptures got in the way of coming unto Christ.

Another lesson that we can learn as we seek to improve our own teaching is what happens when we become overly dogmatic in our interpretations. The Jews of Jesus' day were so convinced of their interpretations that they rejected Jesus. We might take our cue from Jesus, however, who used the scriptures to teach principles, rather than to perpetuate dogmas. At times he also used the scriptures to challenge those time-accrued assumptions.

Jesus and Isaiah

While the purpose of Jesus' ministry was established long before the world came into existence, the substance of what he taught in mortality was not subject to an equal amount of prophetic attention. Some prophets may have envisioned to whom he would teach the gospel (Isaiah 61:1–3), but the principles and subjects that he would discuss were not established before his birth with the same direction and clarity. Instead, the subjects that Jesus discussed were likely chosen through inspiration and revelation, which indicates that Jesus most likely sought that inspiration during his own lifetime. He faced very real human situations and he tailored his message to fit those situations. These important considerations help us realize that, like us, Jesus also considered and pondered what he should teach.

This can be seen practically in the way that Jesus focused on a certain scriptural theme at the beginning of his ministry. At the beginning of his mortal ministry, just as Jesus was preparing to publicize his message, Jesus referred frequently to the words of Isaiah. Something in the wording of Isaiah caught his attention, a focus that also appears in his parables. Isaiah taught, "The Spirit of the Lord God is upon me; because the Lord hath anointed me to preach good tidings unto the meek; he hath sent me to bind up the brokenhearted, to proclaim liberty to the captives, and the opening of the prison to them that are bound . . . to comfort all that mourn" (Isaiah 61:1–2). As in other aspects of his teachings, Jesus appears to have had a special concern for the poor and downtrodden (meek). As he contemplated what he would teach and how he would teach it, he found inspiration for his audience in Isaiah. This must have been a particular concern for him at the beginning of his ministry because the emphasis on Isaiah 61 is later replaced by an emphasis on prophecies of the Messiah's death.

Jesus used other passages from Isaiah besides chapter 61 to describe his ministry. For example, he taught, "And in them is fulfilled the prophecy of Esaias, which saith, By hearing ye shall hear, and shall not understand; and seeing ye shall see, and shall not perceive: For this people's heart is waxed gross, and their ears are dull of hearing, and their eyes they have closed; lest at any time they should see with their eyes, and hear with their ears, and should understand with their heart, and should be converted, and I should heal them" (Matthew 13:14–15 quoting Isaiah 6:9–10).

There may have been several reasons why Isaiah's prophetic words formed the basis of Jesus' scriptural description of his early work and ministry. His audiences may have believed that those same scriptures looked forward to the coming of the Messiah; and therefore, Jesus used those scriptures because they understood them. In other words, the Jews probably did not look forward to a Messiah who would suffer and die, which would have precluded him from using Isaiah 53, but they did look for a Messiah who would rescue the poor and downtrodden, making the reference to Isaiah 61 more meaningful. From the surviving evidence, it appears that Jesus taught his disciples in language that they could understand, even if it meant some more obvious and perhaps meaningful truths remained unmentioned.

One reason why the Lord may have taught from Isaiah, specifically, is that Isaiah did not confuse the Messiah at his first and second comings. In other words, Isaiah kept the mortal ministry of Jesus separate from his later Millennial rule. Many Jews living in Jesus' day believed that the Messiah who would come would be a warrior or powerful king who would return Israel to her former glory. That king, who would be of the lineage of David, would eventually overthrow all oppressors and restore the kingdom to the family of David. Instead, Jesus drew on the following themes from Isaiah's words to clarify some of the popular confusion of his coming:

- Some would harden their hearts against the message, and therefore God would take the truth away from them (Isaiah 6:9–10; Matthew 13:14–15).
- The Messiah's ministry would be foretold by a forerunner (Isaiah 40:3; Matthew 3:3).
- The people of the Messiah's day would draw near to him with their lips, but their hearts would be far from him (Isaiah 29:13; Matthew 15:8–9).

Jesus drew on Isaiah's words because they taught a correct understanding of who the Messiah would be, rather than what some Jews of the first century thought he would be. Interestingly, Jesus did not refer to himself as "The Messiah" or the "son of David," both first-century Messianic terms. Others used those terms to describe him, but he did not apply those titles to himself, likely because of what they had come to mean in the first century. Instead Jesus preferred to refer to himself as the "Son of Man," which had divine overtones (Moses 6:57; Abraham 3:27) but could also mean simply "a son of a man." Unfortunately, even though Isaiah spoke more broadly concerning the Messiah, those chapters and themes that we now find particularly meaningful were not part of the public discussion of Jesus' day, and therefore these passages were not mentioned in Jesus' teachings at least insofar as the Gospel authors remembered them.

In our own teaching we might learn from Jesus' ponderous searching of Isaiah's words for clarification and understanding of his own mission.

Jesus pondered the words of the prophets and drew upon them to answer challenges and convey the message of what he had come to do.

JESUS AND PSALMS

Although the Book of Mormon's quotations of Isaiah make that book the most frequently quoted book of scripture, in the New Testament, Psalms is actually the most heavily quoted Old Testament book. One of the reasons for this is that early Christians drew on Psalms heavily as they began to see Jesus' works and life as a fulfillment of Old Testament scripture. There may have been many reasons why they turned to the Psalms so frequently, but probably the greatest reason was simply that they knew that book of scripture well. The book of Psalms was an ancient hymnal of the Jews and early Christians; therefore they would have been very familiar with its contents.

Jesus himself occasionally drew on the Psalms when teaching of his ministry, although his biographers—the Gospel authors—used it more frequently. One example of Jesus' use of the Psalms is the cry from the cross: "Eli, Eli, lama sabachthani?," which is a quotation of Psalm 22:1. Jesus' explanation of cleansing the temple included a quotation from Psalm 8:2. Many notable prophecies about Jesus' ministry can be found in the Psalms. For example:

- The mockery while Jesus hung on the cross (Psalm 22:7)
- The casting of lots for Jesus' clothing (Psalm 22:18)
- Jesus' cry, "Father, into thy hands I comment my spirit" (Psalm 31:5)
- Judas' betrayal of Jesus (Psalm 41:9)
- The soldiers giving Jesus vinegar to drink (Psalm 69:21)
- The prophecy that the builders would reject the chief cornerstone (Psalm 118:22; Acts 4:11).

Early Christians relied on the book of Psalms to understand Jesus. It provided them with specific and accurate details of who Jesus was and how ancient prophets had foreseen his life of suffering and death.

Perhaps the greatest lessons that we can learn from Jesus' use of the Psalms is that he saw in them a fairly detailed road map of his own ministry, particularly the final week of his life. Prophets had foretold what he would experience and even what he would say. In addition to gaining a greater understanding of Jesus and his life in studying the Psalms, perhaps we can learn from Jesus' example of searching and then teaching portions of the book of Psalms. That road map that he discovered in passages such as Psalm 22 might not provide such a clear road map for us, but the cue to search the scriptures for inspiration and direction in our own lives is certainly a characteristic of Jesus' life that is worth emulating.

JESUS AND EXODUS

To some extent, the Gospel authors and other early Christians understood Jesus as the fulfillment of the prophecies in Exodus and Deuteronomy. Rather than providing the specific wording that would describe Jesus' later actions, the books of Exodus and Deuteronomy provided a metaphor or parallel to Jesus' ministry, in describing Moses. A comparison of Jesus to Moses reveals a striking number of parallels, particularly in the Gospel of Matthew. For example, each of them delivered a new law (Sinai and the Sermon on the Mount), each of them ascended a mount where they spoke with God (Sinai and the Mount of Transfiguration), and both provided food miraculously in the wilderness (the manna and the feeding of the five and four thousand). Both men were saviors and leaders, teachers and prophets. The list of parallels extends well beyond the few mentioned here. But more important than the parallels themselves are the reasons for including them in the New Testament, and what those reasons can tell us about the teachings of Jesus.

Originally we set out to discover how Jesus used the scriptures in his own teachings. The parallels to Exodus and Deuteronomy provide a portion of the answer because they reveal what the earliest biographers of Jesus thought, thus reflecting at least in part what topics were being discussed in Jesus' day and how the early followers understood Jesus. The Gospel authors wrote many years after the death of Jesus, when the story had had time to distill in their minds and hearts, and they saw in Jesus a strong parallel to the ancient lawgiver Moses.

That the authors made such explicit reference to Moses testifies that this was a dominant feature in their understanding and probably also a dominant feature of Jesus' teachings.[3] Moses called Israel out of the world, a feature of Jesus' teachings that corresponds to the Book of Mormon prophecies of his work. Jesus also gave Israel a law and led them into the Promised Land. These ideas may have been in the minds of the

Gospel authors when they wrote, and perhaps Jesus even longed for those parallels to be made between Moses and his own ministry. The parallel to Moses may even have shaped the way Matthew, who recorded more parallels than any other author, told the story of Jesus. Perhaps Matthew also saw Jesus as a lawgiver, a leader, a teacher, and one who would lead believers to a new Promised Land.

Although we cannot be certain that Jesus specifically portrayed his ministry in a way that made the parallel with Moses obvious, we can be safe in following the lead of the evangelists who had this impression of him when they wrote. The parallel to Moses tells us something about his presence and style: he was powerful in the way he taught and clear in the direction he conveyed. The evangelists saw in Jesus a lawgiver and Savior, which helps us see that Jesus presented a strong and clear message. The ability to teach is often proportionate to one's ability to convey a clear message, in this case a message of building up and not tearing down.

Jesus and Deuteronomy

Early Christians used the book of Deuteronomy to draw parallels between Jesus and Moses (Deuteronomy 18:15–18; Acts 3:22–23; 7:37). But more important, Jesus used Deuteronomy in a way that can teach us an important lesson on the value of scripture study. The story of Jesus being confronted by Satan at the beginning of his public ministry is often referred to as the temptations of Jesus. One of the most interesting things about this story is that the Lord responded to Satan by using the words of scripture instead of his own words.

When confronted with the request to turn stones into bread, Jesus answered with a verse from the book of Deuteronomy (8:3). Satan's rejoinder, which in the Gospel of Matthew is recorded as the second temptation, also contains a quotation from scripture. Instead of quoting from Deuteronomy, however, Satan quoted from the book of Psalms (91:11–12), this time confronting Jesus with words that he likely inspired in the first place. Jesus' response came again from Deuteronomy (6:16). How far the issue can be pressed is an important question, but the logic of the interchange between Jesus and Satan does suggest that the latter was at least conversant with scripture. Satan's final challenge to Jesus on that day questioned Jesus' desire to take now what he would eventually receive through obedience. Again Jesus answered using the language of the book of Deuteronomy (6:13).

Each of Jesus' responses to Satan's challenges was framed using the language of Deuteronomy. The reason for this may have been that the book of Deuteronomy contained the law of Israel. Jesus thus responded to Satan by drawing upon verses that formed part of the law of Israel, offering a subtle subtext that Satan's plan, if followed, would break the law. Jesus would not violate that law, even for the immediate pleasures and gratification that Satan offered. More important, Jesus used the scriptures to rebuke and Satan used the scriptures to challenge.

In this brief, scripturally charged confrontation, we learn that Jesus was intimately familiar with the scriptures. He was able to quote scriptures from memory when he was in the desert and without any written texts. That level of familiarity with scriptural wording is certainly a hallmark feature of the greatest teacher.

SUMMARY

Jesus interpreted and used the scriptures in a variety of ways during his mortal ministry. Surprisingly, he rarely used them to teach of his own ministry although he certainly did so on occasion. More often he used them to challenge popular assumptions or to rebuke. Jesus' contemporaries used the scriptures of the Old Testament, particularly the Psalms and Exodus, to understand his mission. Jesus seems to have specifically avoided using the more obvious Messianic scriptures to refer to himself, but instead he allowed his followers to make those connections on their own, probably after his death. Perhaps Jesus knew that greater understanding could be achieved through self-discovery rather than if he had pointed out all the connections.

It appears that one of the lasting impressions Jesus had on his contemporaries is that he was like Moses in many ways. The parallels are both significant and frequent. While the parallels to Moses are and were important, it appears that other ancient prophets turned to Isaiah when studying the life of the Redeemer. Isaiah, more than any other Old Testament prophet, presented a wide perspective on the Messiah's role as Redeemer in mortality, Savior of mankind, Lord of the earth, and Father of creation. Certainly some Isaiah passages specifically referred to Jesus' roughly thirty-three-year lifespan, but the majority have a broader eternal perspective.

In looking closely at Jesus' particular method of using scripture in his teachings we also learn that he was intimately familiar with them, thus testifying to the time he spent studying and pondering their meaning. When confronted by popular misinterpretations of them, he did not shrink from using them to counter the challenge. It is also apparent that he frequently allowed the context of a situation to determine which scriptural truths he would discuss or divulge. With almost endless possibilities at his disposal, he used the existing frameworks of challenge, inquiry, concern, and so forth to determine what he would draw from the scriptures. When his audiences were concerned about Jesus' possible connections to Isaiah's prophecy (Isaiah 61) for example, he did not discuss Isaiah 53 or Psalm 22. Instead he built on their understanding.

Perhaps the most profound summary that can be made of Jesus' use of the scriptures, and the one that will add great strength to our own teaching, is Jesus' clear reliance upon the wording of scripture. The implication that Jesus spent a significant amount of time studying the scriptures is repeated throughout the stories of his life. That time spent studying and thinking about the words of the prophets added depth to his teaching, much as it can to our own teaching.

ATTRIBUTE 6

How a Powerful Teacher Used Prayer

JESUS' PRAYERS AND HIS COMMENTS ON PRAYING AT A GLANCE:

- Jesus criticized hypocritical prayers (Matthew 6:5)
- Jesus used the term *Abba* in his prayers, a word akin to dad or father (Mark 14:36; Romans 8:15; Galatians 4:6)
- He prayed before raising the dead (John 11:41)
- He prayed all night long before he called the Twelve Apostles (Luke 6:12–13)
- He offered other long prayers that lasted much of the night (Mark 1:35)
- He prayed, at least at times, prostrate rather than kneeling (Matthew 26:39)

THE PRAYERS OF JESUS

Several New Testament authors provide glimpses into Jesus' mortal personality, and although they remain only hints, they tell us something about the greatest teacher. One way to view Jesus' personality are the prayers he offered during his mortal ministry. His recorded prayers are indeed few, but they all point to a similar characteristic.

Enos, the son of Jacob, stands out in the Book of Mormon as a man of profound prayer. In fact, he is the only person in the Book of Mormon to have recorded praying for an entire day and into the night. But that was a single occurrence, or at least he mentioned it was on one occasion. Many factors contributed to his offering of a daylong prayer. In his own words he revealed, "I had often heard my father speak concerning eternal life, and the joy of the saints. . . . And my soul hungered" (Enos 1:3–4).

But Jesus did not likely approach prayer with the same concerns that Enos did, or at least he did not do so during his public ministry although he did pray for long periods of time. It may have been that Enos offered a prayer seeking for forgiveness, something that Jesus never sought (Enos 1:2). If the Savior never needed to pray for forgiveness because he was sinless, then what did he pray for? Perhaps the answer will hold a key to unlocking the heavens in our own prayers, particularly revealing something profound about a teacher's prayers.

Jesus' Personal Prayers

We can be fairly certain that Jesus would have prayed during the public prayers and together with his peers at major festivals and holidays. Shortly after Jesus' death, the apostles continued to pray in accordance with Jewish practice as Acts records, "Now Peter and John went up together into the temple at the hour of prayer, being the ninth hour" (Acts 3:1). It would be strange to see the disciples reverting to this practice if Jesus had either condemned it or forbidden his followers from observing it.

Shortly after delivering the Sermon on the Mount to a group of disciples, Jesus created a quorum of Twelve Apostles from that original group of disciples. Certainly that group of disciples was much larger than twelve and would have included men and women, young and old, faithfully committed followers and vacillating listeners. They appear to have primarily come from Galilee. Perhaps they had even heard him deliver the Sermon on the Mount and had witnessed some of the early miracles (Matthew 4:23–24).

Choosing from those disciples to become apostles was not a simple task, especially the head of that group who would eventually lead the followers of Jesus after his death. Although we do not know of their fates with certainty, we have reason to believe that all twelve of the first apostles, with the exception of John the Beloved, died premature deaths.

Essentially, Jesus was singling out twelve men, most of whom would meet a fate similar to his own. One of the twelve would even meet a worse fate than death. As Jesus prepared to call twelve men into his service, "he went out into a mountain to pray, and continued all night in prayer to God" (Luke 6:12). The impression that the Gospels give is that Jesus sought guidance so he could be certain of whom he was calling because the twelve would lead the kingdom in his absence.

The suggestion that Jesus prayed all night in order to receive the inspiration to call the twelve is subtle. The KJV even inserts a paragraph marker (¶) between Jesus' prayer and the calling of the twelve, thus suggesting that the KJV translators considered the two events as separate occurrences. But Luke appears to have joined the two events as he continues on in the narrative, "And when it was day, he called unto him his disciples: and of them he chose twelve" (Luke 6:13). Luke's account suggests that Jesus spent the night in prayer before he called the twelve to serve him.

The importance of this prayer and its connection to our understanding of Jesus is immense. We learn that Jesus was inherently mortal and that he sought inspiration on the night prior to calling the Twelve Apostles. It may be that he sought inspiration concerning whom he should call, or perhaps he pled for the Father to strengthen those who would accept the call. The possibilities of what he prayed for are endless, but the point to remember is that he sought inspiration because he was not immediately omniscient in this matter. Rather it required an exerted spiritual effort on his part to learn the mind and will of the Father or to seek the Father's blessing for the newly called. It is remarkable how quickly he came to the answer. According to the Gospel of Matthew in particular, Jesus had hardly any time to learn anything about the disciples before he organized the twelve. They had only recently gathered into a distinct group that could be identified as disciples rather than simply as followers or interested onlookers. That group of disciples may have numbered in the hundreds, perhaps more.

The Gospel authors provide two slightly different perspectives on how Jesus called his disciples. Luke records that several of the disciples were permitted to see miracles prior to their call to the apostleship. In Luke the process of calling the Twelve is based more on the early experiences that they had with Jesus and on revelation. After Jesus had seen how some of the disciples responded to his teaching and miracles, he sought the inspiration to make the call explicit. In Matthew, the process of calling the Twelve is almost entirely based on Jesus identifying a group of disciples through his early teachings (the Sermon on the Mount) and through a select number of miracles where individual disciples were singled out (Matthew 4:18–25). Matthew does not record Jesus seeking inspiration through prayer. That may be due in part to Matthew's impression that Jesus may have been omniscient (see Matthew 9:4; 12:25) and therefore did not need to seek inspiration.

Gethsemane and Events Leading to It

In Matthew 13 a subtle shift takes place from narrating Jesus' experiences to relating the story of the disciples and how they were beginning to understand whom Jesus was and what he had come to do. This chapter corresponds well with Luke's central section when Jesus works his way toward Jerusalem (Luke 9:51–18:14). One of the events in Matthew's account anticipates Gethsemane and the pain that Jesus would suffer there.

While crossing the Sea of Galilee, the disciples were directed to enter a boat and cross the lake. Jesus promised to come after them, but he remained behind to disperse the large crowd that had assembled as a result of the feeding of the five thousand. According to Matthew, "And when he had sent the multitudes away, he went up into a mountain apart to pray: and when the evening was come, he was there alone" (Matthew 14:23). Matthew then adds that Jesus joined the disciples "in the fourth watch of the night," which would correspond to the early morning hours, roughly between 3:00 AM and sunrise (Matthew 14:25). This would indicate, then, that Jesus had been praying before sundown until early morning, or roughly seven or eight hours. Surprisingly Matthew did not relate what Jesus was praying for, but only that he prayed on that night before he walked on the water. Again, Matthew's interest in Jesus' omniscience may have caused him to overlook the subject of the prayer.

A careful look at Matthew's ensuing story line reveals, perhaps, what he was praying for on that evening. Following Matthew's narrative, John the Baptist had recently died, and the Mount of Transfiguration loomed ahead of Jesus and his disciples. The event also occurred on the eve of Jesus' departure to Tyre and Sidon, both Gentile dominated cities that he would visit, in part, to time his arrival in Jerusalem and to help diminish the persecution against him (Matthew 15:21). With his ministry drawing to a close, and with the disciples nearly ready to receive the necessary keys and priesthood authority that would allow them to lead the Church after his death, Jesus spent the night praying. Although we cannot be certain, it is possible that Jesus may have been praying in preparation for Gethsemane, to steel himself for what was about to transpire. Matthew effectively demonstrated this focus by removing all references to months and years, and thus created a narrative of purpose rather than a historically focused biography.

Although we conjecture that the events of the Mount of Transfiguration took place in late autumn or early winter of the year before Jesus died, we do not know precisely when those events occurred. If this supposition is correct, then just a few months later Jesus again prayed in a way that caught the evangelists' attention. The exact time of Jesus' arrival in Gethsemane and the time of his departure are not noted by the evangelists. But while in Gethsemane, the synoptic account records three separate prayers of Jesus, each petitioning the Father concerning the gravity of the task that lay before him. In each of those prayers, the petition indicates that the actual event is yet future. Only Luke adds a detail that would indicate that the distressing event described in Jesus' petitions had taken place. The anguish of the three petitions is realized in the appearance of an angel from heaven and Jesus subsequently sweating great drops of blood: "And there appeared an angel unto him from heaven, strengthening him. And being in agony he prayed more earnestly: and his sweat was as it were great drops of blood falling down to the ground" (Luke 22:43–44). These verses seem to describe the event that Jesus had anticipated.

Matthew's account of the Garden of Gethsemane indicates that Jesus' prayers in the garden may have taken much longer than the few verses might otherwise indicate. Matthew records that after Jesus' third petition that Jesus "cometh . . . to his disciples, and saith unto them, Sleep on now, and take your rest. . . . Rise, let us be going" (Matthew 26:45–46). There are no events that take place between Jesus saying, "Sleep on now" and "Rise, let us be going." Luke's words, however, suggest that there was a significant temporal break in the story, where an angel visited Jesus and he sweat great drops of blood. Luke only knew that in that moment when he was in great pain, he "prayed more earnestly" (Luke 22:44). Like his prayer while the disciples were crossing the Sea of Galilee, Jesus appears to have been deeply engaged in praying and that his earnest pleadings began to take a toll on his physical body. While in that condition, he sought the inspiration of heaven to resolve the matter, or perhaps to bring it to its purposeful conclusion. The answer to that prayer did not come quickly, and when the answer came, it crushed Jesus as Luke depicts.

One interesting note is recorded concerning Gethsemane that is not recorded in the telling of the other stories: Jesus prayed while lying prostrate: "And he went a little further, and fell on his face, and prayed" (Matthew 26:39). The position in which he prayed was even noteworthy to the evangelist Matthew. The visual image is of a person crushed by an incredible weight or a person experiencing severe pain and suffering.

SEEKING TO BE ALONE

The Gospel of Mark records that Jesus, "rising up a great while before day, he went out, and departed into a solitary place, and there prayed" (Mark 1:35). Mark does not connect this story to the preceding or following narrative, but instead includes it in passing without any particular focus. In considering this event, several details stand out that are similar to other events in the Savior's life, perhaps indicating a certain personality trait. According to this brief passage, Jesus sought a "solitary place" where he could be alone. On at least six other occasions Jesus sought solitude in a "desert place" (Matthew 14:13; Mark 1:45, 6:31–32; Luke 4:42, 9:10). So, for example, "Jesus could no more openly enter into the city, but was without in desert places" (Mark 1:45); "When Jesus heard of it, he departed then by ship into a desert place apart" (Matthew 14:13); "And when it was day, he departed and went into a desert place" (Luke 4:42). In all of these examples the same Greek word is used, sometimes translated as "solitary" but often as "desert." In fact, this adjective is used more than any other in the Gospels to describe Jesus' physical surroundings. Jesus sought solitude and quiet to be alone or at least be away from the throngs of people. Sometimes the disciples followed him, but in many instances, he simply sought to be alone.

Another detail from his life confirms Jesus' reflective and pondering personality. Near Jesus' hometown—Nazareth—and near the cities where he ministered, there were large Roman era cities with all the trappings of Greek (Hellenistic) and Roman culture. These cities, Tiberias, Sepphoris, and others, were large metropolitan centers that offered jobs, luxuries and amenities, and goods for sale. But surprisingly the Gospels never mention that Jesus entered into them. Instead he reserved his ministry for very small Jewish villages located primarily around the Sea of Galilee.

To show this, it is helpful to note that at the time of Jesus, the population of Sepphoris has been estimated to be around 12,000 people and that of Tiberias to have been slightly smaller, perhaps between 6,000 and 12,000 people.[1] Although not large by modern standards, these were the two largest cities in the region where Jesus taught. By comparison, Jesus taught in very small cities, with many of them having populations less than 2,000 people. Cities like Bethsaida, Capernaum, Cana, Chorazin, Bethany, and others were quite small. Jesus appears to have preferred the smaller cities; some of them very small even by the standards of his day. These subtle suggestions indicate that Jesus sought solitude, frequently preferring to be alone and away from the crowds. From the evangelists' impressions of him, it appears that he had many things on his mind, and that he sought quiet opportunities to pray. Those prayers, the evangelists remembered, would stretch long into the night.

We might surmise that Jesus was at times a solitary, reflective individual who spent long hours in prayer on the eve of important and life changing events. We cannot know the words of his prayers and whether they focused on the struggles of self or on the future of the kingdom and its disciples. But perhaps most important, the greatest teacher prayed frequently and sought quiet moments to reflect. In many ways the Gospels have given us the impression that he even preferred rural cities and small gatherings of people.

PRINCIPLES OF PRAYER

Jesus' first recorded prayer came after the question, "Lord, teach us to pray, as John also taught his disciples" (Luke 11:1). Luke then records the prayer now known as the Lord's Prayer. The Gospel of Matthew records a very similar prayer but in a very different and earlier context. He records that Jesus taught his disciples and followers the Lord's Prayer during the Sermon on the Mount (Matthew 6:9–15). Perhaps the differences in these two prayers indicate that they actually represent two separate teaching instances, a subject we will address at greater length shortly.

At the time of Jesus, believing Jews would participate in prayer three times a day, at morning, midday, and in the evening. At the morning and evening prayer they would recite the words of the Lord to Moses found in Deuteronomy 6:4–7.[2] In the afternoon, Jews in Jerusalem would stop to pray when they heard the trumpeters from the temple signal the time. That prayer would be a personal request for forgiveness of sins and the wording of which may have been spontaneous. In fact, Jesus may have had in mind those who offered such prayers when he condemned the public prayers of the hypocrites. In rural Galilee the practice of daily praying for forgiveness in the afternoon may have been modified, or perhaps the practice was less public, which may in part explain why Jesus' condemnation of the practice is so pointed: it stood out to him when he traveled to Jerusalem.

So how were Jesus' prayers viewed in light of common first century practices? Of course, there were differences, but for the most part Jesus' prayers were similar to those of his contemporaries except in a few instances. On one occasion, however, he taught what can be referred to as the principles of prayer: principles that should guide the prayers of his followers in their daily lives. Those principles of prayer that he taught were not revolutionary in their contextual setting, but they offered guidance for personal spontaneous prayers.

The wording of the Lord's Prayer in Matthew is: "Our Father which art in heaven, Hallowed by thy name. Thy kingdom come. Thy will be done in earth, as it is in heaven. Give us this day our daily bread. And forgive us our debts, as we forgive our debtors. And lead us not into temptation, but deliver us from evil: For thine is the kingdom, and the power, and the glory, for ever. Amen" (Matthew 6:9–13).

Beginning with a recognizable and simple introduction, Jesus expresses the idea that the Lord is our Father and that Jesus' relationship with him is like our own relationship with him. He called on him saying "Our Father" rather than saying "My Father." Later, after the resurrection, Jesus told Mary Magdalene, "But go to my brethren, and say unto them, I ascend unto my Father, and your Father; and to my God, and your God" (John 20:17). That later saying supposes that Jesus' relationship to the Father was different after the resurrection. However, during his ministry Matthew remembered that Jesus spoke to the Father in the same way that we do. He pled for the Father's help as we continue to do today. We learn from this the first principle of prayer: the sanctity of the Father's name. Jesus prayed that the father's name might be kept holy, thus directing the remainder of the prayer to include petitions that would achieve that end.

In his second petition, Jesus taught a principle of prayer that was not so much a contradiction of Jewish practice but rather a contradiction to human nature. When we pray, we find ourselves in a paradox of asking an omniscient and omnipotent being to recognize our human will and to grant certain things based on perceived needs. Here Jesus commends his followers to make the divine will our own will rather than trying to convince God that our will should be his will. The word *thanks* does not appear, but the principle focuses on the recognition of God's hand in our lives, something we learn to be thankful for through humility.

The third principle, "Give us this day our daily bread" is the first item asked for in the prayer: enough food for that day but no more. Luke realized the difficulty created by such a request when we ask only enough for that day but do not consider the next day or the day after that. Subtly, he changes the phrase to read, "Give us this day our daily bread day after day" (Luke 11:3; author's translation). Jesus' statement as recorded in Matthew does not exclude the possibility of being blessed with food for the coming days, but he did not specifically ask for it.

The fourth principle (and the one for which there is a significant difference in wording between Matthew and Luke) is the idea that our forgiveness is intricately intertwined with how we forgive others. Rather than asking God to simply forgive us, Jesus taught that forgiveness is dependent upon an action. But instead of offering righteous works or obedience as a proof of that action, Jesus taught that the necessity of forgiving others of their debts to us was a precondition to God forgiving our debts.

Luke makes the connection between debts and sins explicit by changing the word "debts" to "sins." And while the word in Matthew can mean "sins," it more often refers to an obligation that is owed to someone. The principle remains the same in Matthew's and Luke's versions, but the wording in Matthew is more inclusive while Luke offers a more specific application. Although we cannot be certain that the original situation did not lead to the difference in wording (the Sermon on the Mount versus a question that the disciples asked), it does appear that both Luke and Matthew were attempting to understand the meaning of what Jesus had said.

The final petition of the prayer leads to a doctrinal predicament because here Jesus petitions the Father not to lead mankind into temptation, something that we would not expect the Father to do (see James 1:13–14). The JST changes the active verb into a passive construction,

"And suffer us not to be led into temptation" (JST Matthew 6:14), thus allowing Satan to be the author of temptation and the Father to control the extent of it. The Greek word *tempt* employed by Matthew derives from the same root as the verb used to describe the temptations of Jesus in Matthew 4 as well as the title used of Satan, "the tempter." The word, however, can also mean "trial" or "test," which may reflect what Jesus said in Aramaic more closely when he petitioned the Father not to lead us into trial or into a test rather than the KJV's "temptation."

To draw out the lesson from the Lord's Prayer, let's reflect back on the previous chapters where we have seen Jesus' preference for teaching principles instead of commandments. But there is more to be gleaned from this passage. In Jesus' day prayer had become something very public and rigid, and here Jesus subtly corrected the popular thinking on prayer and turned it into a very private event, reflecting his own prayers that took up nearly an entire night. As teachers we might benefit from a renewed effort to make the Lord's will our will rather than trying to make our will his will.

Abba

Very few of Jesus' actual words are recorded in the New Testament or anywhere else. What we do have are extensive translations of his words. In essence, the Gospels have preserved primarily how Jesus' Aramaic words were interpreted and translated into Greek. In many instances it would be immeasurably helpful to know the exact words that Jesus said, but instead we are forced to rely on Greek translations of what he said.

So, the few words that Jesus did speak that are preserved in the Gospels in Aramaic stand out as unique and intriguingly different from the other words of Jesus. Why they were preserved in their original form is not known with certainty, but they stand out as examples of Jesus' personal mode of speech.

Frequently, the New Testament records that as Jesus prayed or spoke to God the Father, he addressed him personally as "Father" (see John 11:41; 17:1). The Greek text records the simple noun *father* without any capitalization or underlining. It is the same word that a person would use in referring to his or her own mortal father. On a later occasion, Jesus also referred to the Father as El, using the singular instead of the plural (Elohim) of that same noun that is common today. In that singular instance, while he hung on the cross, the wording of that invocation came from Psalm 22:2.[3]

Privately while he was alone in Gethsemane, Jesus appears to have addressed the Father using the phrase "Abba," a word that could be translated as dad or father: it envisions a father-son relationship between the person saying it and the person being spoken to (Mark 14:36). The term *daddy* is probably too familiar to describe the meaning of Abba. The New Testament provides its own translation of the word when it includes the word *Father* after each reference, providing a translation of the word as the Gospel authors understood it rather than the exact wording Jesus used.

Christians were so fascinated by Jesus' usage of the term *Abba* that they continued to remember it and to use it in their own prayers. Using that term would have seemed strange given the more formal relationship that Jews had envisioned existing between them and God. God the Father had become so removed from ordinary affairs that either shortly before or shortly after the birth of Jesus they began to shun even pronouncing God's name. Jesus' prayer offered a striking contrast. Not only did he speak to God using the Father's name, but he also referred to him affectionately using a familiar term.

Jesus' language of prayer, at least the term *Abba*, shows us that he felt close to the Father, using ordinary speech that any son would use of his father. The close relationship that Jesus felt with the Father may demonstrate to us a similar need to rely on the Father, as a close advocate and instructor.

SUMMARY

Unfortunately, the New Testament only records a few passing references to the prayers of Jesus even though the greatest work he ever performed began with an earnest prayer in the Garden of Gethsemane. The few recorded prayers of Jesus reveal that he sought occasion to be alone, sometimes directing his disciples to travel ahead of him so that he would have an opportunity to pray and be alone. At other times the disciples were nearby when he prayed. Although the Gospels only record Jesus' longer prayers, sometimes taking the entire night, his shorter prayers were not recorded because they were likely similar to those offered by others in his day. The Gospel writers noted the different prayers, those that seemed unusually long or pointed.

Jesus also taught during the Sermon on the Mount some important principles of prayer. The principles he taught are simple and straightforward. It requires less than a minute to read the prayer through in its entirety, which is perhaps why his longer prayers stand out as so intriguing. Jesus' principles of prayer continue to shape the way we pray today. For some they provide an exemplary prayer, so eloquently offered that it should be repeated. For others, the words of the Lord's Prayer provide guidance in how we seek inspiration and revelation from an omniscient Father who already knows our needs and desires.

Great teachers are often contemplative people who consider all aspects of a subject before presenting any thoughts upon that subject. To be a great teacher, one must know the subject matter well. For Jesus that meant he had to know the subject well (we saw in the previous chapter that he was intimately familiar with the scriptures). In this chapter we have seen that he prayed long hours during the days and nights prior to some of the great events of his life. With this detail and the way Jesus sought solitary moments, we begin to see more fully into the heart of the world's greatest teacher.

ATTRIBUTE 7

Remaining Humble Despite Being Great

TITLES OF JESUS AT A GLANCE:

- The title "Son of Man" was used of Jesus eighty-four times (eighty-three by Jesus himself) and is the most common way that Jesus spoke of himself.
- Jesus never referred to himself as the "Christ" according to the Gospels and the later epistles, although many called him that and he did not deny it.
- Some of Jesus' enemies were fond of calling him Jesus of Nazareth, probably because they thought it emphasized that he was not from Bethlehem, the city of David.
- Followers of Jesus called him the Son of God on twenty-eight occasions.

THE SON OF MAN AND OTHER TITLES OF JESUS

One of the disadvantages of historical perspective is that it often obscures our ability to ask the right questions of our sources. For example, for us Jesus is the Christ or Messiah, a fact confirmed through faith and restoration scripture. And yet, Jesus never referred to himself as the Christ in the New Testament. In fact, one of the great differences between the two halves of the New Testament—the Gospels and letters—is that the title Christ is used sparingly in the biographies of Jesus where we would expect the term to have been discussed; however, it appears frequently in Paul. The title appears fifty-eight times in the Gospels in reference to Jesus, but is never used by Jesus to refer to himself. This title is used 464 times in Acts through Revelation, all in reference to Jesus. In fact, it is used so frequently of Jesus that it appears to be a name (Jesus Christ) rather than a title (Christ Jesus or Jesus the Christ). So we might conclude that people believed that Jesus was the Christ, but that Jesus never referred to himself that way or that the Gospel authors did not remember him to have spoken in that way. That is not to suggest that Jesus was not the Christ or that he did not believe that he was the Christ, but instead it may signal a humble approach of the master teacher in handling his own spiraling reputation and power.

Great teachers often become great celebrities and are sought after frequently. Those teachers face the difficult challenge of managing that celebrity status and maintaining the love and passion that brought them to their subject in the first place. As that challenge develops the other challenge of using credentials to build credibility and popularity also arises. Teachers want to cite the books they have written or draw attention to academic credentials. But in Jesus' case, he was confronted at times with large crowds that believed in him and at other times with small gatherings that were hostile to him. In either of those cases, or many more like them, he could easily have declared himself to be the Creator, the Savior, the Messiah, or any of the other titles that describe him. But had he done so, would such a declaration have jeopardized his own quest to be humble?

Evidence of how Jesus spoke of his ministry or referred to himself is surprisingly straightforward, but also quite different than what we might initially anticipate. The issue is made difficult because Jesus often would not respond to questions of where he came from, where he was born, whether he really was a son of Joseph, or other antagonizing questions meant to demean him. He held his peace on those occasions, and so some of the titles used of Jesus are difficult to understand in their historical context. On those occasions when he was challenged, we might expect him to offer clarifying answers indicating his role as Messiah or his divine parentage. When others called him the Messiah, we might expect him to frequently endorse that declaration. However, this was often not the case.

When considering the titles that Jesus used to refer to his own ministry, something stands out that certainly applies to our own human desires to seek worldly recognition. Jesus had the most impressive credentials that anyone could aspire to. He is the Son of God, the Messiah, the King of Kings, the Savior. The list could go on! Jesus certainly did not lack proper credentials, yet he did not make claims based on those credentials. When we look at how Jesus spoke of himself, we can see profound humility in his character. When he answered criticisms, he chose to humbly safeguard his own credentials and focus on the doctrinal issue at hand.

Negative Titles

Certainly people called Jesus names in his lifetime: to suppose otherwise would be suppose that he did not share in the common experiences of mortality. The New Testament hints only at a few of them. Perhaps the oldest slander about Jesus (Jesus of Nazareth) has been passed down to us in the form of a title. Today it appears to be part of a name or title that was given to Jesus; and, in fact, is sometimes used favorably in the New Testament even though it may have a negative origin. However, the New Testament texts also hint that this apparent name developed in circles that were unfavorable toward Jesus.

The title "Jesus of Nazareth" is never used in the second half of the New Testament (Romans through Revelation), the oldest portion of the New Testament, a testimony to the fact that Jesus' earliest followers preferred to use the more divine titles such as Lord and Christ. And Paul, the earliest writer to ever mention Jesus in any way, never used that title to refer to Jesus in his surviving epistles. When the title is first used—the first time occurs in the Gospels—it appears in situations where it is used favorably of Jesus. In one instance a person who is healed of a demon cries out, "Let us alone; what have we to do with thee, thou Jesus of Nazareth?" (Mark 1:24). Nearly contemporary with this event, Philip reported to Nathanael that he had found "Jesus of Nazareth" (John 1:45). Both of these examples derive from the early part of Jesus' ministry, one of them even prior to Jesus' public teachings. In both of these instances the title seems to have circulated prior to the start of Jesus' teaching ministry, perhaps from the time when people only knew him as an artisan from Nazareth. Because Jesus was such a common name in the first century, it may be that the title was at one time used to distinguish him from the many other men named Jesus in his day much like Magdalene, or a person from Magdala, distinguished one Mary from all the others.

But a further look of this title also shows it is typically used in a negative context in the Gospels. When Jesus' antagonists spoke to him or about him, they did so in a limited number of ways. First, they preferred to call him Jesus and not the Son of Man as he preferred to speak about himself. Second, they derisively called him Jesus of Nazareth, a title that Jesus never used. Third, they explicitly rejected the idea of a Messiah from Galilee. Nazareth was in the heart of Galilee, so calling him Jesus of Nazareth may have been one way to emphasize that he was not Jesus of Bethlehem.

Some examples show that the title Jesus of Nazareth was often, if not always, used negatively by Jesus' opponents. When the party of temple police, Roman soldiers, and Pharisaic guides came to arrest Jesus, they inquired after "Jesus of Nazareth," thus indicating that this particular title was the way some of Jesus' opponents in Jerusalem spoke about him (John 18:5, 7; Mark 14:67). This party did not know Jesus personally nor did they recognize him when they saw him, so they had to inquire who he might be. But interestingly they knew that he was called Jesus of Nazareth. It appears that they spoke about him in that way when they planned to arrest him. It would be very natural for them to seek to avoid using the positive titles such as Christ, so as not to worry those who were uncertain in their attitudes about Jesus.

Pilate also had this inscription written on the cross so that people would know exactly who Jesus was specifically. Simply writing "Jesus" on the cross was not enough information to distinguish him from others. When Peter was waiting outside the palace where Jesus was being interrogated, a young woman said, "This fellow was also with Jesus of Nazareth" (Matthew 26:69–71). All of these examples attest that common people and the authorities in Jerusalem referred to Jesus as Jesus of Nazareth, and in particular that Jesus' antagonists used this title to distinguish him. They did not refer to him as the man who claimed to be x or y, but rather they preferred a lowly title with no pretensions of greatness. The title was particularly popular among Jesus' antagonists in Jerusalem. Surprisingly, calling him Jesus, the one who thinks that he is the Christ, would have been very disparaging, but the title Jesus of Nazareth was sufficient for his detractors.

This very title reveals many things by what it does not claim, and although any argument from silence can only yield tentative results, some hints support the following suggestions. Some common people, at least, did not know him as the Son of God, the Son of Man, Jesus Christ, Jesus the Christ, or any of the other important titles that his followers used. Instead, he bore an ordinary name and came from an ordinary town in Galilee. Interestingly, however, we know that people had heard of him—from the maid who sat outside of the home of the high priest to those who questioned Nicodemus' fledgling faith. And in all of these examples, they had heard of Jesus through channels that were likely opposed to him. All they knew was Jesus had some physical association with the small Galilean village of Nazareth.

In one story in particular, a subtle hint conveys that title may have been used negatively. While in the city of Jerusalem, a controversy arose among some of those who had heard Jesus teach. Some claimed, "This is the Christ. But some said, Shall Christ come out of Galilee?" (John 7:41). The issue or point of concern was whether a man named Jesus of Nazareth (in Galilee) could be the Messiah. Some Pharisees launched a more official inquiry into the matter and rejected Jesus outright. During those proceedings they declared, "Search, and look: for out of Galilee ariseth no prophet" (John 7:52). So the title Jesus of Nazareth, at least from the middle of his ministry onward, began to carry a stigma that he was *not* Jesus of Bethlehem or Jesus the Christ; he was the ordinary Jesus from Nazareth, which meant that he could not be the expected Messiah.[1]

Matthew 12 envisions a time when some of the people of Galilee had begun speaking ill of Jesus: "And whosoever speaketh a word against the Son of man, it shall be forgiven him: but whosoever speaketh against the Holy Ghost, it shall not be forgiven him, neither in this world, neither in the world to come" (Matthew 12:32). Although the KJV translation translates the passage as "whoever speaketh," the verb in Greek conveys the idea that the act of speaking against Jesus was still ongoing. The phrase might also be rendered as "whoever might speak," or "whoever would speak" against the Son of man. The Greek translation, which hopefully follows Jesus' wording in Aramaic, implies that Jesus is not referring to a specific event when someone spoke against him or even a specific individual who had spoken against him; rather, it seems to imply that Jesus knew of slanders that were circulating about him at the time he was speaking.

Interestingly, Jesus' statement accepts the fact that some may have circulated rumors or slanders about him, yet he understood that they would be freely forgiven of such misinformed statements. Jesus here was clearly following his own teachings not to refer to one another using the derogatory "Raca," a word that means something akin to "empty," or "worthless" and by implication, "empty headed" (Matthew 5:22). It would have been easy for Jesus to refer to those who had spoken ill of him using such negative terms, an approach that may have even generated a laugh from his audience, but he refrained and instead taught what things they could say that would not be forgiven. In other words, he taught principle rather than react to their name-calling (Matthew 12:32). Again, his response to those who slandered him shows a remarkable degree of restraint and poise as he remained focused on being the Messiah rather than proving that their assumptions were incorrect.

POSITIVE TITLES

On a variety of occasions, people referred to Jesus using a title that was partially generated through biblical prophecies of the Messiah's coming and partially through the popular hope that the Lord would send a deliverer to Israel who would free them from Roman oppression. Biblical passages referring to the Davidic ruler or Messiah who would overthrow the enemies of God's people are abundant (see 1 Chronicles 17:11–14; 2 Samuel 22:44–51 [Psalm 18:44–51]; Psalms 2:2–6, 7–9; 89:3–4, 20–29; Isaiah 9:7; 11:1–10; Jeremiah 23:5–6; Ezekiel 34:23–24; 37:25; Amos 9:11–12). Piecing together these passages to create a harmonious picture of a triumphant Messiah who would end Roman domination in Galilee and Judea was a natural consequence of a believing people who looked to the prophets and law for instruction.

When Jesus began to teach in rural Galilee and Judea, accepting crowds sought to understand him. The foundation of their understanding came through their understanding of the Bible, and it was natural for them, given the conditions they were living in, to suppose and hope for the immediate coming of the Messiah. Indeed, when they referred to Jesus as the "Son of David," it reveals a belief in him and his ability to end their oppression and sufferings. In fact, the connotation is that they accepted Jesus as a temporal Savior. They seem to have appreciated, at least in part, his message that he had come as God's emissary in the world (see John 14:6).

But according to the Gospels, Jesus never referred to himself as the "Son of David" nor did he ever encourage such a designation. Whether he scoffed at the notion or whether his silence was a tacit acceptance of the identification is no longer clear. However, the term appears most often in the New Testament as a subtle reminder of the genealogical authority of Jesus. It came from the lips of those who had been healed by Jesus, and therefore as a declaration of flattery and their acceptance of Jesus as a deliverer.

When two blind men sought Jesus and asked him to "have mercy on us," they called him the "Son of David" (Matthew 9:27). Again, when Jesus had healed another man who was blind, the people questioned, "Is not this the son of David?" (Matthew 12:23). And a woman, who lived in Sidon, well outside the borders of Galilee, called Jesus, "O Lord, thou Son of David" (Matthew 15:22). Jesus was referred to or thought of as the Son of David on six separate occasions (Matthew 1:1; 9:27; 12:23; 15:22; 20:31–32 [Mark 10:47–48; Luke 18:38–39]; 21:9, 15; Luke 3:31), and in the earliest Christian writings, the epistles of Paul (see Acts 13:22; Romans 1:3). Jesus never endorsed this title, and in fact, he continually directed his followers to see other aspects of his ministry.

People referred to Jesus in a variety of other ways also. The Gospel of John implies that in a select few instances, Jesus either taught that he was God or was equal to God (John 10:30; John 14:10–11, 20; John 16:15). The examples are always subtle except for the two instances where he is recorded as saying "I am" (John 8:58; 18:6, 8). At other times, Jesus either taught or people thought of Jesus as the Messiah (Matthew 16:20; 24:5; Mark 13:6; Luke 21:8; John 4:25–26; 17:3), the Bread of Life or the Bread of God (John 6:33–35, 48, 51); the Lord of the Sabbath (Matthew 12:8; Mark 2:28; Luke 6:5); the light of the world (John 8:12; 9:5; 12:46), the door (John 10:7, 9), the good shepherd (John 10:11, 14), the way, the truth, and the life (John 14:6), the resurrection and the life (John 11:25), and the vine (John 15:1, 5).

But each of these last examples represents a singular event or a very limited application of a specific title. People did not consistently think of Jesus as the Messiah or the Bread of Life, for example. Jesus did not repeatedly use those phrases in reference to himself. Instead, Jesus taught about his own ministry in two very specific ways. Above all else, Jesus referred to himself most often as the Son of Man. Either he, or his followers, used that title on fifty occasions amounting to eighty-three occurrences in the

Gospels. The second most important way that people referred to Jesus was as the Son of God, which occurred on twenty-eight occasions, although Jesus used the title for himself only on four occasions in the Gospels. We should also include all of those instances where he referred to God as "my Father," but those instances could be misinterpreted as references to a mortal father even by his followers.

As we considering the titles that others used for Jesus, we see how they were attempting to understand him as well as dispel confusion of what he had come to do. We can also see how Jesus sought to manage his own identity. Many thought of him as a son of David, one who would end oppression. Some of Jesus' discourses may have resulted from him trying to clarify that while he was the Messiah (see John 10:1–6; 14:1–6), he had not come to end Roman domination. He encouraged belief in his life and ministry, even though at times those who declared their belief were not fully aware of who he was.

As we explore the theme further, we will see how Jesus described his own ministry in some detail. But at this stage, it is important to note how he carefully guided his followers away from thinking of him in ways that described his role at the Second Coming (like the Son of David) and toward his real mission (the Son of God). He could easily have built a base of followers using such exalted and ennobling titles such as Messiah; instead, Jesus was humble and preferred to teach principles rather than taking the glory prematurely that was based on an incomplete understanding.

THE SON OF GOD

When Jesus Christ began preaching the gospel of repentance in Galilee and Judea, he often referred to himself as the Son of God. The title itself is simple and enigmatic at the same time because the words are easy enough to understand but their implication is not. Mark entitles his work, "The beginning of the gospel of Jesus Christ, the Son of God" (Mark 1:1) suggesting that for him the title, when considered alongside the other divine title—Christ—epitomized Jesus and his teachings. To complicate matters, however, we must recognize that Greeks understood sons of god to be a race or class of men who had a divine and mortal parent. These children of Zeus or the Olympian gods were sometimes great and sometimes tragic characters. It is possible to assume that when Mark called

Jesus the Son of God he meant something like what the Greeks meant because Jesus also had a divine and mortal parent.

In the Old Testament, the sons of God took wives from among the daughters of men. Their offspring, it is often assumed, are the giants mentioned in the same passage, leading some to believe that the sons of God in this passage refer to the angels (Genesis 6:2–4). Later, in the book of Job, the premortal spirits who meet with God to present themselves are similarly called the sons of God (Job 1:6; 2:1; 38:7). Important for this chapter is what Mark meant when he referred to Jesus as the Son of God and how that helps us understand his teaching practices on the way to improving our own ability to teach the gospel.

Scripturally the phrase looks back to Jesus' baptism when the Father declared the sonship of Jesus, "This is my beloved Son, in whom I am well pleased" (Matthew 3:17). Effectively, the relationship that the Father declares shows both a profound love for and acceptance of Jesus and what he has been doing. It contains a divine stamp of approval for what Jesus had done, and the voice of the Father would lead us to look forward in hope that he would continue to be pleased with Jesus' work

From what we can surmise from the writings of Jesus' contemporaries, it is not entirely clear how Jesus' listeners would have understood the title Son of God, but it appears to have its origin in the natural human longing to be with God and be accepted into his family.[2] In calling Jesus the Son of God, his followers likely recognized him as blessed and accepted of God, something that they would have desired for themselves also. They may have even considered the full ramifications of the title as we do today. The message of acceptance and divine approval shines through in the Father's statement at Jesus' baptism. We might express the same sentiment today by describing someone as blessed, accepted of God, or loved of God. That seems to describe the way people looked at him: something about him made people assume that he was blessed and loved, perhaps even one of God's special sons as the contemporary literature describes the term. And for us now, we learn how Jesus allowed people to grow in their understanding of him rather than explaining all the details immediately and explicitly.

Jesus' patience and longsuffering still stands out as Jesus developed a clear picture of who he was and what he had come to do. With his followers, he did not abruptly correct incomplete understanding nor did he seize the opportunity for premature grandeur.

JESUS THE SON OF MAN

The title Son of Man appears more frequently in the Gospels than any other title about Jesus.[3] It is used eighty-four times (eighty-three by Jesus himself), although it appears only four times in the second half of the New Testament, three of them in reference to Jesus. Certainly there has been a significant discussion about what the title means today and what it meant at the time of Jesus. Usually those discussions focus on Moses 6:57 and its reference to the "Man of Holiness . . . and the name of his Only Begotten is the Son of Man." But those definitions help us see what the believers in Jesus might have understood, and in particular, they help us see, through the lens of the Restoration, what Jesus might have meant when he spoke of himself as the Son of Man. Unfortunately, Jesus did not explain the meaning of the term nor did he apparently use the phrases found in Moses 6:57. We might rightly ask what his followers would have understood when Jesus used the Old Testament title "Son of Man." Would his followers have associated the term with the son of man prophecies in Daniel, or would they have understood something akin to what has been revealed through modern scripture? Perhaps they understood him to mean something different still. And there is the possibility that in using titles to refer to his own ministry, that some would have thought him to be arrogant. It is important to look at the impact of using such a title in the first century, how others would have responded, and what claims were being made by using it. In discovering answers to these questions, we will see whether it was a humble declaration, a statement of power and position, a clarification, or something else entirely.

A few consistent patterns emerge in Jesus' use of the title "Son of Man." First, when Jesus referred to aspects of his own salvific life and death, he would typically refer to the work of the Son of Man as though it were someone other than himself. For example, Matthew reports this prophecy, "For as Jonas was three days and three nights in the whale's belly; so shall the Son of man be three days and three nights in the heart of the earth" (Matthew 12:40). In the Gospels, we are taught that the son of man had power to forgive sins (Matthew 9:6), was Lord of the Sabbath day (Matthew 12:8), would return in his kingdom (Matthew 16:28), and would be betrayed into the hands of wicked men (Matthew 20:18). Many other important details of Jesus' ministry are also revealed through the use of this title.

No doubt Jesus used the title to refer to himself even though he used it in third person. On a number of occasions, typically to the disciples alone, he made the connection explicit. He asked the disciples at Caesarea Philippi, "Whom do men say that I the Son of man am?" (Matthew 16:13). On an earlier occasion, Jesus performed a miracle in which he interpreted his own actions as being those of the son of man. He told his audience, "But that ye may know that the Son of man hath power on earth to forgive sins, (then saith he to the sick of the palsy,) Arise, take up thy bed, and go unto thine house" (Matthew 9:6).

For Jesus, the title Son of Man defined who he was and what he had come to do, but for his antagonists, they preferred to use more confrontational titles as noted above. Had the title simply meant a son of a human, as the Greek words could easily imply, then it would be odd that his opponents did not pick up on such an inferior title and use it against him.

The uses of the title may help explain what Jesus' contemporaries thought of it when they heard him speak of the Son of Man. Perhaps the most important feature of the Son of Man prophecies is that they permitted Jesus to speak frankly and openly about his ministry in front of crowds and even hostile audiences in a way that would not increase persecution. Jesus' antagonists in the Gospels were already sensitive to his self-declarations and some felt that his claims bordered on blasphemy (see John 10:31). By using the title Son of Man, Jesus said things that were much more provocative and straightforward than he might have said had he used his own name. This may also explain why he never explicitly referred to himself as Jesus the Christ while others openly did.

Using the title also permitted Jesus to explain the role of the Son of Man on earth and how his life would be offered on behalf of others. The vast majority of the Son of Man sayings deal with the issues of the Atonement and the Second Coming. These teachings touched upon sensitive doctrinal subjects and may have created undue and premature opposition to Jesus, thus inhibiting him from completing his mission as he had planned to do.

By speaking of himself as the Son of Man, Jesus also gave his followers and later disciples ample time to assimilate who he was and what he had come to do. As the portrait of the Son of Man began to take shape in their minds, Jesus carefully made it clear that he was that Son of Man. Had those teachings been delivered in complete clarity from the beginning of his ministry, Jesus may have been dismissed as a crackpot

Galilean upstart. Even today, those who claim to be the Messiah, or God, or some other divine figure are almost universally ridiculed and dismissed. Some may have still followed him, but it gave many the opportunity to accept all that Jesus was teaching without the difficulty of accepting that Jesus would accomplish those deeds.

Finally, the title probably appeared as a humble self-declaration to those unfamiliar with the biblical text. Whether in Aramaic or Greek, the words meant something like "a human" or a "certain person" (see Psalm 8:4; Ezekiel 2:1 for examples of the ordinary use of the title). It could carry more grandiose overtones, and it could be interpreted biblically, but for many it would simply mean a person. That Jesus used this rather ordinary term to teach the basic outline of his ministry is telling in that it reveals a subtle correction of popular belief. Like modern Christians today, Jews expected a triumphant deliverer, one who would restore the glory of Israel and right the wrongs inflicted upon them. There were many nuances to this developed understanding of the Messiah's role, but the basic outline was similar among many who looked forward to his coming. The Jews looked for someone to save them, and that someone was almost certainly conceived of as a divine figure.

Instead of openly advocating a different position, teaching that the common assumptions were misguided and confused, Jesus humbly taught that a human, a specific individual, would bring to pass the Atonement of mankind. That same human would return in glory in a kingdom that was not of this world. Furthermore, that human would suffer, die, and be disregarded by the people. This Son of Man would do many of the things that the Jews expected in a deliverer, but he was human and seemingly ordinary. Jesus humbly built up a worldview of what the deliverer really was and what he had come to do without using confrontational language. He was humble when he taught about his own ministry, and his teachings about the Son of Man must have had familiar ring to them because they drew on imagery of a Messiah that would triumph in a different way.

Like many other master teachers, the titles that Jesus used of himself reveal his ability to deliver a message on multiple levels. He taught profound truths about the ministry of the Son of Man, and privately he testified that he was that Son of Man. Ironically it was by claiming a certain title for himself that Jesus was able to deflect some of the criticisms of self-proclamation. Although many titles that others used for Jesus may have been true, Jesus limited the ways he spoke about his own ministry.

Summary

The Gospel authors remembered that people derided Jesus and referred to him in derogatory ways. The trend in first century Galilee and Judea was to emphasize Jesus' humanity, pointing out that he was an ordinary person from Nazareth and that his father and mother were known as were his brothers and sisters (Matthew 13:55; Mark 6:3). They challenged him on other points as well, choosing to think of him as a Galilean upstart with Messianic pretensions. If the Pharisees could successfully create a public impression that Jesus was a fraud or crank who had deluded himself, then they would have won the battle for the hearts of the people.

But as they sought to publicly discredit Jesus, he subtly taught that the ministry of the Son of Man would rectify the situation through suffering death and a glorious return. His hesitance to fight back reveals a profound personal humility. The Son of Man would save mankind, and initially it would have been easy to assume that Jesus was referring to another individual who was yet to come. As the tensions between Jesus and the Pharisees escalated, Jesus made the identity of the Son of Man known to his followers and his antagonists. With the basic outline of the Son of Man's ministry in place, his followers could watch its prophetic fulfillment take place in the life of Jesus. His teachings were masterfully crafted and delivered in a way that captured the imagination of a people who looked for redemption. The Son of Man sayings also reveal a person of profound humility, one who carefully guarded his divine identity until his followers were ready to receive it. He also did not use his authority or the calling as Messiah to demean and belittle his antagonists, even though they were challenging and mocking God's anointed servant.

Jesus was the Son of Man in a proper sense, and in the way that the Restoration teaches (see Moses 6:57), but if our sources are accurate for his lifetime, then it is safe to assume that no one in the New Testament considered the title in the way that we do today. The New Testament authors offered a different vantage point, one that teaches that the Son of Man teachings were used in part to advert undue persecution away from Jesus.

Perhaps the most important New Testament title used for Jesus is not the Son of Man, but rather the Son of God. This title must have developed in circles where followers could overlook the slanders about Jesus not being divine. The title speaks to the very essence of who Jesus was and not necessarily to what he did or accomplished. Accepting a mortal as the literal Son of God was a powerful testimony to their faith and acceptance of Jesus.

ATTRIBUTE 8

Learning Empathy

The temptations of Jesus at a glance:

- Prophets living hundreds of years before Jesus saw that he would be tempted (Alma 7:11; Isaiah 53:4)
- The Gospels record that Jesus faced three temptations, but then do not record any other temptations
- Jesus' encounter with Satan in the Judean wilderness is the only recorded encounter between the two during Jesus' mortal ministry
- Although they do not specify why, Matthew, Mark, and Luke understood that the temptations were the event that prepared Jesus to begin his ministry

The Temptations of Jesus: Understanding Human Experience

Perhaps no other surviving story reveals so much about Jesus' personality, inner concerns, and private trials as do Matthew's and Luke's accounts of the temptations Jesus faced at the end of a forty-day fast. The Gospel of Mark passes over the story briefly, mentioning, "And immediately the Spirit driveth him into the wilderness. And he was there in the wilderness forty days, tempted of Satan; and was with the wild beasts; and the angels ministered unto him" (Mark 1:12–13). Unlike Mark's account, Matthew and Luke each devote nearly an entire chapter to tell the story and place it squarely among the other formative experiences that Jesus had prior to the beginning of the public ministry. More than any other narrated scene from Jesus' life, the temptations provide a glimpse into a time when Jesus became like us. Certainly there were many other earthly experiences that brought him close to us, but interestingly those stories are rarely hinted at or narrated in any detail. The gospel writers could easily have told stories from his early family life, of his emotions at the loss of a friend or loved one, of his physical stature and abilities, or even of his own private life. But they chose not to, and instead they told one story that looked deeply into the personality of Jesus of Nazareth.

TEMPTATION: A TRAINING GROUND
FOR THE GREATEST TEACHER

Although perhaps redundant to mention, it is important to note that there were no eyewitnesses to Jesus' temptations except for Jesus himself and Satan. No other witnesses are implied or mentioned, and therefore, we must assume that the accounts we now have were revealed months or years later to faithful disciples and followers. Perhaps Jesus made reference to them in his discourses.

If the accounts of the temptations can be traced back to Jesus or through inspiration of the Spirit, then it is also very likely that the wording of the stories reflects, at least in part, the way that he spoke of the event and wanted it to be understood. This is important because the stories are conveyed in a way that suggests a genuine temptation rather than a simple test that was easily overcome: the stories reveal a genuine struggle. When recounting the stories, the Gospels of Matthew, Mark, and Luke all used a verb that can refer to a "test or trial" or in a negative sense it can also mean a "temptation."[1] At the heart of the matter is whether Jesus was genuinely tempted to do the things Satan tried to entice him to do, or whether he simply shrugged them off as misguided attempts to bring about his fall. Certain clues in the story as well as doctrinal insights provided by ancient and modern prophets will help answer this question.

Another matter of historical and doctrinal importance about the temptations is that numerous prophets mentioned the event both before and after Jesus' lifetime. Prophets prior to Jesus' life mentioned the Atonement, miracles, birth, and baptism, which typically are considered the most important events of his life. But prophets also spoke about his temptations, thus attesting to the comparative importance of this event in the life of the Savior. King Benjamin referred to the temptations (Mosiah 3:7) as did Abinadi (Mosiah 15:5), Alma made reference to them while at the same time quoting from Isaiah who also appears to have foreseen the temptations (Alma 7:11; Isaiah 53:4), Paul made reference to them in Hebrews (Hebrews 4:15), and the temptations are mentioned in the Doctrine and Covenants (20:22).

That prophets saw the temptations of Jesus and considered their doctrinal significance many years before the Savior was born, underlines how important they are for understanding the ministry and meaning of Christ's life. These experiences shaped him and the way he taught. In fact, they form part of the very foundation of who Jesus is and was. Both Matthew and Luke include accounts of the temptations and place them prior to the beginning of the mortal ministry. For some reason, according to at least two of the Gospel authors, Jesus was not fully prepared to begin his mortal ministry until he had been baptized *and* tempted.

TRYING TO CREATE CONTENTION

In our everyday experiences, we learn that contention either minimizes our effectiveness to hear the promptings of the Spirit, or it simply drives the Spirit away from us. As a subtext to the temptations of Jesus, the struggle of wits between Jesus and Satan appears, at least initially, aimed at encouraging a dispute and thus allowing a contentious spirit to develop.

Satan first challenged Jesus by saying: "If thou be the Son of God, command that these stones be made bread" (Matthew 4:3). Ironically, Satan devised the test and what it would prove, which if completed successfully would prove not that Jesus was the Son of God, but rather from a believer's standpoint that he had fallen from his position as Messiah. But at least on one level the test probed Jesus to determine whether he would respond out of pride or turn away. It also offered Jesus an opportunity to prove himself to someone who was attempting to provoke him. He reminded the tempter, "It is written, Man shall not live by bread alone, but by every word that proceedeth out of the mouth of God" (Matthew 4:4).

Jesus' response was carefully chosen from scripture (Deuteronomy 8:3). Instead of using his own words to rebuff Satan, he chose words that had been revealed to Moses. This carefully chosen answer avoided the trap that Satan had set by reducing the chances that the confrontation would escalate to the level of angry rebuttals. Literally, his answer teaches that man should focus on what comes out of his mouth rather than what goes into it. Jesus may also have been doing that very thing, that is, guarding himself in how he responded.

Further mocking Jesus, Satan offered a second challenge to Jesus, this time interweaving his wording with scripture. He quoted directly from Psalm 91:11–12, but offered a twisted interpretation saying, "If thou be the Son of God, cast thyself down" (Matthew 4:6). Certainly the original meaning of Psalm 91 was mutilated in Satan's rendering of it. What he wanted to know was whether the Father would stop the Son from doing something that would jeopardize the Atonement if the Son were to choose to do so. Would the Father save the Son's life to rescue the Atonement? Jesus responded by quoting from Deuteronomy 6:16: "Ye shall not tempt the Lord thy God." Surprisingly he did not say yes or no, but rather Jesus directed Satan to stop tempting God. Although we cannot be certain of whom Jesus meant when he referred to God, it is possible that he was reminding Satan that he should not tempt the Father to send angels to rescue him. Or perhaps Jesus even meant that he should not tempt God, that is Jesus, to do something contrary to the plan.

Satan's attempted confrontation fizzled when Jesus refused to enter the fray with him. He could easily have become frustrated at Satan's misuse of scripture, his limited foresight, and his sarcastic question. But Jesus remained firm in his response, again choosing to answer using the words of scripture rather than his own words in the moment of confrontation.

Finally, Satan offered to Jesus something that he could genuinely give, at least for a short time. He offered to Jesus the kingdoms and glory of the world without the pain of the Atonement. But certainly Jesus knew that eventually in taking those things he would lose them eternally. Again he answered by calling on the words of the prophets, quoting from Deuteronomy 6:13. At its most basic level, each of the temptations were delivered with challenging, sarcastic overtones, begging Jesus to fight back and defend himself and his beliefs. Each of the temptations incorporates the word "if" in them, and each attacks from a different angle. But unfortunately for Satan, Jesus remained poised, calm, and ready to respond to his harshest critic. If Jesus was nothing else in his life, he was certainly calm in the face of mockery.

Satan's challenge, however, may have been more pointed than initially appears; while it is easy to see that one of the desired results was to cause Jesus to respond with anger, the actual threat of doing so may have been more substantive than the temptation stories record. In one of the most provocative verses in the entire New Testament, the Gospel of Mark records, "And when he had looked round about on them with *anger*" (Mark 3:5; emphasis added). Mark describes Jesus' anger using a word that could be translated as "wrath, anger," or "indignation" (Greek has no way of distinguishing between divine anger—righteous indignation—and human anger or wrath).[2] According to Mark, Jesus became angry, or at least he appeared to do so. Although modern sensibilities dictate that being angry violates the commandments, the law of Moses does not prohibit anger and thus Jesus could be angry and not violate the commandments.

A second incident, much like the incident where he appeared to be angry, occurred at nearly the same time, and again suggests that Jesus may have exhibited an emotion that appeared to be frustration or even anger. In this example Jesus had entered a home and because of his popularity, a throng of people attempted to follow him inside. Apparently the crush of people became so great that they could not move inside the house, "so that they could not so much as eat bread" (Mark 3:20). While in these cramped quarters Jesus was "beside himself" (Mark 3:21), which in Greek is literally rendered as "out of one's mind" or "troubled." Exactly what Mark was attempting to convey with these words is not entirely clear and Matthew and Luke do not tell the story in the same way.

Whatever happened on that day, according to Mark, some of Jesus' friends assumed that he had become very emotional and that they needed to rescue him from the situation, or at least they believed that he needed help. Again, the subtle suggestion is that Jesus at times showed strong emotion, perhaps bordering on anger (Mark 3:5) or that he exhibited emotions that made him appear deeply passionate (Mark 3:21). In any case, we cannot know exactly what Jesus felt on those two occasions, but we do know what Mark and perhaps others thought about his moods. It is possible, even likely, that Satan saw something similar in Jesus' character and attempted to exploit it by causing him to lose his temper or to press him in his emotions.

Today we assume that Satan knows our weaknesses and exploits them in his diabolical attempts to deter us from following the Lord. As we consider our plight and the possibility of tailor-made temptations, we might also consider that the same rules of mortality applied to Jesus. If there was indeed a weakness, then Satan would certainly seek to exploit it to his advantage. Our first hint of any weakness appears in the temptations: Satan tried to entice Jesus into an argument (a challenge repeated on numerous occasions during the mortal ministry).

THE SECOND CHALLENGE:
USING THE PRIESTHOOD APPROPRIATELY

At the heart of the temptation stories lies the issue of whether they tempted rather than what they tempted, but in learning what aspects of Jesus' character they tempted, we can also see whether Jesus was *genuinely* and *thoroughly* tempted. Learning another's temptations seemingly opens a window directly into that person's soul because it reveals their innermost weaknesses and challenges. When we know a person is weak in something, somehow we believe that we can understand and define that person. For a moment, the Gospel authors have permitted us such a glimpse into the personality of Jesus even though we remain cautious in using the words weakness and challenge.

A note on how we might answer this challenging issue is also in order. No one ever recorded that Jesus spoke of his temptations throughout his life, nor did they indicate that he reflected on the seriousness of the temptation. But a few clues recorded at various times throughout the gospel narratives indicate that some of the issues raised during the temptations continued to challenge Jesus in new ways during his life, thus suggesting that Satan continued to challenge him to commit sin in areas where Satan perceived a personal weakness. Those later challenges reveal a consistent temptation to do certain things, some of which Satan seemed to be aware of during his forty-day fast and ensuing challenges.

Satan offered to Jesus a simple paradox in his first temptation. Jesus, who had the power to do so, was asked whether he would use his priesthood to bless himself, or whether he would wait longer and find food at an appropriate place to end his already lengthy fast. The wording was simple, the challenge direct.

In relationship to what Jesus actually felt during the temptations, Matthew records what is perhaps the most ironic statement in the Gospels: "And when he had fasted forty days and forty nights, *he was afterward an hungered*" (Matthew 4:2; emphasis added). Avoiding any symbolic interpretation of the event, which Matthew, Mark, and Luke also avoid, we might surmise that Jesus was not simply hungry but starving. Perhaps Jesus taught it in that way, revealing what he felt at that moment—genuinely hungry.

But the most challenging question, whether Jesus would use his priesthood to bless himself or satisfy his personal physical needs, appears tailored to Jesus. Not long after the temptations, while traversing the Sea of Galilee, some of the disciples became concerned that their small boat would soon sink in a raging storm. They awoke Jesus who immediately calmed the storm (Matthew 8:23–27). Nothing that Jesus had said or done prior to that day could prepare them for such a great miracle: he had healed persons afflicted with disease, but he had never changed the course of the weather. Before his rebuke of the elements Jesus said, "Why are ye fearful, O ye of little faith?" (Matthew 8:26). But this rebuke is precisely contrary to what the disciples had asked of Jesus. They asked, "Save us: we perish" (Matthew 8:25). What more could they ask of Jesus?

And yet the story reveals something about Jesus' personality. Had they known that Jesus could not die on that ship on the Sea of Galilee on that day, because such a death would not be an atoning death, they would have realized that their chances of reaching the shore safely were fairly certain. Although they might die in that storm, Jesus could not die in that particular storm. But how could they have known that much about Jesus when he had not taught them those things according to the evangelists? Rather, the story reveals that Jesus again faced a challenge that raised the question of whether he would use his priesthood to save himself. In this case he saved others, but this continued line of thinking leads to an interesting thought: perhaps Jesus was faced with this very temptation throughout his life as Satan continually pressed the issue. In this example, the fine line between saving oneself and saving others through the priesthood is indeed thin, perhaps intentionally so, because Satan wanted to dissuade Jesus from his mission.

A similar type of challenge arises in the stories when hostile crowds sought to do bodily harm to Jesus. A subtext of the many attempts to stone Jesus or otherwise do him harm is the power of priesthood. Jesus could easily have used his priesthood in those instances to save himself, whether through miraculous delivery or through other means. It seems that Satan continually pressed Jesus on this point, giving Jesus ample opportunity to ask himself whether he would misuse the power God had given him if the circumstances became too dire. The true depth of this challenge is only appreciated as we recognize that Jesus genuinely had the power of God at his command, and that he could have attempted to change the course of events had he so desired.

THE THIRD CHALLENGE: JESUS' BELIEF IN HIMSELF

Satan pointed out to Jesus in his second temptation a simple paradox. If Jesus was the Son of God, would God the Father stop him from doing something that would jeopardize the Atonement, or perhaps closer to the original wording, would the Father stop Jesus from dying prematurely if Jesus did something foolish like jumping off a cliff (Matthew 4:6). In the second temptation Satan twisted scripture and created an illogical conclusion based on a contrived test. Somehow if Jesus jumped and God stopped him from doing so, then Jesus would be the Son of God.

At first glance, this might appear to be the most misguided of the three temptations. It is simple, and the holes in Satan's logic are enormous. Yet, because Satan used it, it may reveal something that genuinely tempted Jesus. The irony of genuine temptation is rarely so obvious in reality.

A few hints in the Gospels reveal that this was possibly a legitimate temptation of Jesus, and that perhaps he thought seriously about how he would fulfill scripture and what the Father's role would be in his life and death. We do not know what Jesus knew of his future role as Savior. He may have known every detail, or he may have not anticipated anything until the time grew much closer. As mentioned in a previous chapter, it is certain that Psalm 22, which spoke of his death, was of particular concern during the last weeks of his life, but those same concerns and references are not apparent earlier in his life.

What we do know is that during the same time period Jesus was pondering the meaning of Isaiah 61, which taught about his ministry. Later in his life, he appears to have considered the prophetic elements of the Psalms.

We do not know when Jesus came to understand the full scope of his ministry, but he did live in a day when Jews expected a variety of different Messiah figures. Many, but not all, placed their hopes in a redemptive

Messiah who would free them from foreign oppression. In that heated environment, Jesus began to reflect upon a ministry to the poor and downtrodden as envisioned by Isaiah. He would teach them, and thus fulfill the word of the Lord to Isaiah, but did he understand that his calling would lead to the salvation of not only the poor but also all of God's children? Satan tried to interpret that humble ministry in more grandiose terms, suggesting that no matter what Jesus did, God would save him and direct his ways.

The Fourth Challenge: Premature Awards

Jesus, like the majority of his countrymen, taught that obedience was part of the Lord's plan and law to his people. Therefore, if one remained obedient, one would be blessed in the hereafter. And while there were many different conceptions of what the hereafter would be like, Jesus' life of obedience prior to the temptations would have earned him exaltation in the life after death. At the moment that Satan offered his third challenge, Jesus had successfully rebuffed the tempter and had lived a life of perfection. He would achieve exaltation. Satan offered what was likely Jesus' greatest temptation. He asked whether Jesus would accept immediate recognition for his actions or whether he would wait for exaltation and eternal recognition that would only come through paying a terrible price.

The answer seems easy. But no one can fully appreciate what Jesus experienced on that day because no one can anticipate ever feeling that much pain on behalf of others. Satan wanted to know if immediate acknowledgment would be enough of a deterrent to cause Jesus to forget his mission. Jesus, of course, refused the offer and then moved on toward a life that would lead to his sacrificial death. But the temptation would occur again, thus suggesting that it may have been among Jesus' greatest temptations.

Although we do not know much of Jesus' life prior to the temptation stories, it appears that his greatest challenges came at a time when his physical body was weakened. On that day, Jesus faced three great temptations and successfully overcame them. At a later point in Jesus' life, when he was again physically weak but emotionally strong, the third temptation arose again. This time Satan was nowhere to be seen, or at least the Gospel authors were unaware of his presence, but the temptation occurred in Jesus' thoughts and perhaps even in his heart.

After entering the Garden of Gethsemane, Jesus prostrated himself on the ground and began to pray to the Father. The image we can see is of a person who has been crushed through an overwhelming trial and who has been forced to lay prostrate through a physical collapse. In that compromised state, Jesus considered another way. How briefly he considered it is impossible to know, but he asked, "O my Father, *if it be possible*, let this cup pass from me: *nevertheless not as I will*, but as thou wilt" (Matthew 26:39; emphasis added).

Like the temptation stories, the Garden of Gethsemane is a revealing account. No one was awake to see all that happened there. In telling the details of that event, whether through the Spirit or personally, the Lord used the words "not as I will" in reference to Jesus' plea. He had another will, but he accepted the Father's will. The suggestion is subtle and may have amounted to nothing more than Jesus' will being to do the will of the Father, but in light of the third temptation, it is possible that he was indeed tempted to consider the offer.

In our modern dispensation, the Lord reflected again on that very moment and revealed that the pain was intense, so intense in fact that it was a deterrent. He said to Joseph Smith, "How sore you know not, how exquisite you know not, yea, how hard to bear you know not. For behold I, God, have suffered these things for all, that they might not suffer if they would repent; . . . Which suffering caused myself, even God, the greatest of all, to tremble because of pain, and to bleed at every pore, and to suffer both body and spirit—*and would that I might not drink the bitter cup, and shrink*" (Doctrine and Covenants 19:15–16, 18; emphasis added). Even two thousand years later, the Lord reflected on the other way, and while accepting the Father's will, he commented upon the depth of the pain he felt in accepting the Father's will.

SUMMARY

By looking at the temptation stories in this chapter, we are ready to learn several important lessons from the life of the Master Teacher. First, it is important to remember that Jesus was tempted and taught his disciples and the evangelists, who later recorded the stories about Jesus' temptations. All great teachers stand tall both during and after facing temptation. Second, Jesus was tempted and remained sinless. That he was tempted is an important part in gaining empathy. Third, the temptations prepared him. Unlike so many of us, who grow a little in our faith and then face severe temptation, Jesus was tempted before he ever began his ministry. Certainly there are reasons for this, and certainly Jesus' faith was not simply in its infancy. However, the temptations proved that he was ready.

President Howard W. Hunter summarized Jesus' temptations with the following reminder, "It is important to remember that Jesus was capable of sinning, that he could have succumbed, that the plan of life and salvation could have been foiled, but that he remained true. Had there been no possibility of his yielding to the enticement of Satan, *there would have been no real test, no genuine victory in the result.* If he had been stripped of the faculty to sin, he would have been stripped of his very agency. . . . He was perfect and sinless, not because he had to be, but rather because he clearly and determinedly wanted to be" (emphasis added).[3]

It is difficult to consider the moments when God was tempted to be something other than God. All eternity hung in the balance during those brief moments, but the resulting victory was and is monumental. In those moments of humanity, we learn of a man who was like us in some respects. He felt true human emotions, which caused him to consider following a mortal path rather than the divine plan.

Above all, the Gospels record very few events where Jesus is actually like us. He may have appeared like other men, but those who knew him considered him to be different in many ways. He had a divine parent, he seemed increasingly clear on what he was supposed to do with his life (at times the evangelists thought that he was omniscient), he performed numerous miracles, and he taught in ways that were different than other teachers of his day. But the Gospel authors preserved brief accounts of a few instances where Jesus acted like us. They knew of times when he appeared angry, they knew of times when he spoke of his mission and how it affected their lives, and they knew that he faced a considerable challenge during his life. That challenge, to save mankind through excruciating pain, made him more like us than almost anything else he did in mortality. But the Gospels also remind us that this was just a part of his life and that, in the end, he triumphantly succeeded in overcoming temptations.

ATTRIBUTE 9

⬥

Teaching with Humor and Irony

Jesus' Use of Humor at a Glance:

- The Gospels do not attribute any distinctly sarcastic remarks to Jesus.
- Following the Gospels of Matthew, Mark, and Luke, it is apparent that Jesus was fond of using hyperbole when he taught followers.
- Some remembered that Jesus could ask difficult questions (Matthew 22:41–46), while others remembered that he had a sharp wit (John 10:30–39).
- A few of Jesus' teachings appear to be intentionally humorous or dramatic (Matthew 7:3–5).
- People laughed at Jesus, but the Gospels do not record that Jesus ever laughed (Mark 9:24).

HUMOR AND IRONY IN THE TEACHINGS OF JESUS

Humor is a conditioned response and its definition changes across cultures and over time. What some people find funny is often not funny in other cultures; and to say that something is humorous today is often a personal interpretation of what we find amusing rather than what another audience found amusing. Humor is something for which we gain a sense. Rarely do the authors of the New Testament employ a consistent sense of humor. They may point out ironies or paradoxes, but they do not present the life of Jesus in ironic fashion or in exaggerated form. However, Jesus frequently used forms of expression that we might find humorous today, and it may well have been humorous even in his day.

Although Jesus' use of irony and humor in his teachings has been looked at infrequently, it nevertheless remains an important part of the way he presented his message. Modern teachers frequently employ humor in their presentations, and indeed a teacher that uses humor is often more delightful to listen to. We live in a world where people want to be entertained, which is an important component of public discourse. In fact, in the modern era one of the features that distinguishes us from our counterparts in the first century is our appreciation of humor. Our most cherished teachers are also the most entertaining.

But in the first century, particularly in Judea and Galilee, teachers rarely used the types of humor that we use today. Instead, they relied on irony and hyperbole to express their ideas and concerns. Paradox was a common feature of rabbinical teachings. These forms of humor are still recognized today, but another method of teaching that is today often considered inappropriate for some audiences—sarcasm—does not appear evident in Jesus' teachings, although to be certain, we need to distinguish his intent, which is rarely possible given the nature of our texts. Today we distinguish between sarcasm (in our popular culture, sarcasm is the lowest form of humor or wit) and irony. Although sarcasm and irony are probably not distinguishable in ancient texts, for this chapter we should distinguish between the two according to their intent. In both forms the author says one thing but means the exact opposite. In sarcasm, however, the author's intent is seen as derisive and mocking, whereas in irony the intent is dramatic emphasis. Jesus used these forms mentioned above— irony, hyperbole, and paradox—but in the cases where he used irony, it will be important to consider intent. In Jesus' day there was no prohibition against using sarcasm, and this form of humor, which is looked down upon in our day, may not have been viewed so negatively in Jesus' day.

As we consider Jesus' use of humor in his teachings, perhaps we will also find an appropriate balance between humor and substance in our own teachings. Too much reliance on humor means a sacrifice of content, and a teacher that is too serious runs the risk of losing an audience's attention. It is a fine balance indeed, and Jesus' teachings provide us with a few clues on how to achieve that balance.

PARADOX

Jesus used paradox frequently in his teachings; in fact, it was one of his primary means of deflecting confrontation. Some of the paradoxes he employed were subtler than others, while some that were put to him seem to border on being confrontational. For example, late in the Savior's ministry the Sadducees came to him with a riddle concerning the resurrection of the dead. Our surviving historical sources record that the Sadducees did not believe in the resurrection, and therefore they likely asked an intentionally difficult question intended to show their mental or doctrinal superiority to show that resurrection was a fallacy. The question was probably intended to prove that the idea or doctrine of resurrection was inherently illogical. To prove their point, they had carefully constructed a riddle that drew on the idea of levirate marriages, when a living brother was required to marry another sibling's spouse in the event that the first sibling died childless. They challenged how God might sort out such marriages in the hereafter. The riddle was intentionally confusing, and we need not assume that it was created specifically to test Jesus.

When the Sadducees came to Jesus with this question, they likely had been successful in forcing an answer to their riddle in other situations. They may have asked simply to have their curiosity satisfied. The Sadducees were generally devoutly religious and saw themselves as the correct and accepted followers of God. And they followed the biblical injunctions given to Moses quite closely. They accepted it as binding and inspired. So rather than answer their question directly (in the case of a levirate marriage, who would remain married to the first man's spouse in the resurrection) Jesus used paradox to challenge their assumptions. He said, "Ye do err, not knowing the scriptures, nor the power of God" (Matthew 22:29).

Certainly the Sadducees had read the scriptures, they likely assumed they knew them, and they certainly believed that they were God's people. They, like others of their day, felt that they were the chosen people of God and he was saving them. The question was not whether the Sadducees knew of the scriptures, but rather how well they understood them. In fact, they thought that they knew them so well they could use their own understanding of them to challenge Jesus. But Jesus' statement points out that the scriptures do teach of the resurrection; and he implies they did not know them as well as they had assumed. In fact, the opposite was true. Certainly such a strong suggestion would not pass by unnoticed.

The Sadducees were challenging Jesus on a specific interpretation that reflects their own knowledge of the biblical text. According to the New Testament, one of the only surviving historical sources to tell us about the Sadducees, they were at times extreme in their interpretations. Telling such a person that they did not know the primary text under discussion is akin to encouraging a confrontation or asking for a fight. The further paradox in Jesus' statement is that he told them they also did not know or comprehend the power of God and his ability to raise a person from the dead. Their understanding of God's power, Jesus implied, limited his ability to carry out his work, something that they would certainly have taken issue with also.

In this story, where Jesus' antagonists attempted to draw away his followers by showing what they perceived to be an interpretive gap in Jesus' teachings on the resurrection, he used paradox to circumvent their attempt. Jesus' use of humor was on par with the challenge of the Sadducees. Their question appears intended to undermine Jesus' teachings, and his humor undermined their hoped-for triumph.

Perhaps a day or so earlier, as the Gospels report, in a confrontation with the chief priests and elders, Jesus used a similar form of humor, although this time as a conclusion to a parable. After delivering the parable of the householder who owned a vineyard and rented it out to husbandmen, Jesus asked his audience what should be done to those who had abused the master's servants and eventually killed the master's son. The answer was obvious, perhaps too obvious. The leaders answered accordingly, "They say unto him, He will miserably destroy those wicked men, and will let out his vineyard unto other husbandmen, which shall render him the fruits in their seasons" (Matthew 21:41). Couching his response in biting humor, Jesus said to those same leaders, "Did ye *never* read in the scriptures" (Matthew 21:42; emphasis added). Of course they had, and of course they revered those scriptures. But they did not understand them in the same way that Jesus did, and he pointed that out in very challenging language. Again, suggesting to a devoutly religious leader that he had never read the scriptures is akin to inviting one to a duel. Matthew dryly notes, "And when the chief priests and Pharisees had heard his parables, they perceived that he spake of them. But when they sought to lay hands on him, they feared the multitude, because they took him for a prophet" (Matthew 21:45–46). They wanted to kill him because he had challenged them publicly and because they apparently had not offered or been able to offer a response. Although the confrontation was certainly humorous and Jesus used a type of humor in responding to them, no one (except perhaps his followers) seemed to find his answers funny.

One way that Jesus used humor was to counter his opponents when they attempted to lure him into a scripture bash or confrontation. In each of these stories, his antagonists were attempting to gain momentum in their quest to turn public opinion against Jesus, but Jesus used humor successfully to turn the tide or maintain the upper hand. At least some of his humor was not intended to maintain audience interest, but rather to deflect hostility.

IRONY

Unfortunately, it is difficult to determine irony in Jesus' sayings because tone of voice, expression, and body language play such an important part of irony, and we cannot know these things from our surviving sources. Some of his humor was intended to challenge; apparently, he answered in kind when people sought to discredit him publicly. But the most profound irony of Jesus' ministry does not derive from what Jesus said, but rather it was something that one of the New Testament authors noticed.

In the Gospel of John, beginning in chapter 3, a variety of people seek to understand Jesus and who he was. The inquirers range from Nicodemus (a Pharisee) to a foreigner (the Samaritan women). John carefully places these stories alongside one another, each story re-asking the question of who he was and showing how people reacted to him after hearing him teach. But John also realized that a divine irony was playing out in the life of Jesus as this occurred, because, as he noted, "the Holy Ghost was not yet given; because that Jesus was not yet glorified" (John 7:39). With the withdrawal or withholding of the Holy Ghost, it is not a surprise that some found it difficult to believe in Jesus. Ironically, people may not have overcome that difficulty fully in Jesus' life. They could know him, but the fullness of the Spirit was somehow less than it had been or would be in other dispensations. Although it was Jesus who taught about the

121

withdrawal of the Holy Ghost, it seems that John realized the irony of the statement.

In the central section of John's focus on witnesses to Jesus, he also records a saying of Jesus that is made even more ironic when we understand that the ministry of the Spirit had somehow been limited. Without the gift of the Holy Ghost, Jesus' audiences were required to understand Jesus visually through his works, audibly through his teachings, and intellectually through their understanding of the scriptures. Toward the end of his discussion about witnesses to his ministry, Jesus offered the following ironic conclusion, "Search the scriptures; for in them ye think ye have eternal life: and they are they which testify of me" (John 5:39). The NRSV renders the same passage as follows, "You search the scriptures because you think that in them you have eternal life," and thus captures the irony of Jesus' statement.

Jesus was not directing his audience to go and search the scriptures, but rather pointed out that they had indeed searched the scriptures and believed that in the scriptures they had found eternal life. Because of their interpretation of the scriptures, however, they had missed the point that they testified of Jesus and his mission. They did not see the need for living witnesses. The irony was that they had indeed used the proper source, but they had missed their witness of the Savior, perhaps in part because of the limited role of the Holy Ghost. As we saw earlier, in those situations when Jesus' audience profoundly misunderstood him or misrepresented him, he chose to teach principles rather than engage in the spirit of conflict. In this instance, however, he used irony after he taught the principle of witnesses.

HUMOR

One of the hallmark differences between a first century teacher and a teacher today is the use of humor to entertain an audience. We often expect it today. But in Jesus' day, the few times that he used humor, it appears that his audiences did not comprehend it fully.

When Nicodemus came to the Savior at the beginning of the mortal ministry, he enquired concerning whom Jesus was and what he had come to do. Like anyone who meets someone who believes himself to be some great divine personage, Nicodemus treated Jesus as though he were mentally unstable, assuming Jesus believed he was something other than a man from Galilee. The Gospels do not note a sarcastic tone in his voice, but the literalness of Nicodemus' questions suggests that he may have been probing to understand how profoundly confused Jesus really was.

At least initially, Jesus appears to have taught Nicodemus in a straightforward manner, answering his questions simply. He said, "Verily, verily, I say unto thee, Except a man be born again, he cannot see the kingdom of God" (John 3:3). But Nicodemus did not treat the statement as a simple declaration of rebirth or renewal. Instead, he offered a highly sarcastic retort: "How can a man be born when he is old? can he enter the second time into his mother's womb, and be born?" (John 3:4). Many have sought to see Nicodemus' answer as a conditioned response inspired by Jewish literalness or rigidity, but that cannot explain the profound misunderstanding in his approach. Several obstacles confront this conclusion.

First, Jesus, according to the Gospel of John, did not literally say, "Except a man be born again" but rather he said, "Unless a man be born from above" (author's translation). The KJV translation uses the phrase "born again" because it anticipates Nicodemus' response, not because it accurately conveys the meaning of the Greek. Instead, the story contains a sense break. Jesus taught Nicodemus about a heavenly rebirth or renewal—probably alluding to baptism and birth through the Holy Ghost—and Nicodemus misinterpreted him (intentionally?) to mean something grotesquely literal. But the two ideas do not logically follow one upon another unless Nicodemus misunderstood the idea of renewal to mean again.

The second issue is that Nicodemus appears to be treating Jesus a certain way because of the miracles that have been seen by his colleagues or reported to them by others who had seen them. Nicodemus reports, "Rabbi, we know that thou art a teacher come from God: for no man can do these miracles that thou doest, except God be with him" (John 3:2). Nicodemus was hesitant to express belief in Jesus, or even to make the logical conclusion based on his own statement, namely that Jesus is of God. Instead he says, "we know" rather than "I know" or "I believe." Further, he states that the miracles indicate God is with the man who does such miracles, but he did not say that God is with Jesus because he had done those miracles. It is an abstraction, a carefully worded conclusion that if confirmed might indicate that Jesus was of God.

So the hesitant inquirer appears to have been suggesting to Jesus that there was a way to prove himself; he could confirm the hypothesis by doing a miracle or by witnessing how he had done the miracles. And indeed, Jesus taught him how he had done them: he had been born from on high. Unfortunately the New Testament rarely reveals the vocal intonations of a speaker, and in this case, whether it was because of the way Jesus said it or because of the implications of what he said, Nicodemus treated his answer as though it revealed a mental shortcoming.

In response, Jesus first answered the question specifically ("Except a man be born of water and of the Spirit, he cannot enter into the kingdom of God. . . . Marvel not that I said unto thee, Ye must be born again" [John 3:5, 7]) and then used irony or humor. He said to Nicodemus, "The wind [spirit] bloweth where it listeth, and thou hearest the sound thereof, but canst not tell whence it cometh, and whither it goeth: so is every one that is born of the Spirit" (John 3:8). Certainly Jesus' answer is true, but it paints a very different portrait of the Spirit than we are accustomed to thinking about. The Spirit is something like the wind, which you can hear but cannot see, and when it arrives you can feel it, but you cannot determine which direction it comes from or which direction it is going. In other words, it is an uncontrollable phenomenon.

In a day and age when we speak of the environment of the Spirit, or inviting the Spirit, it is difficult to understand this answer. But the clue to understanding it comes in the following lines as John records them, "Nicodemus answered and said unto him, How can these things be? Jesus answered and said unto him, Art thou a master of Israel, and knowest not these things?" (John 3:9–10). We can read Jesus' response in several ways, but the most probable, it seems, is that Jesus was teaching Nicodemus that for people like him the Spirit was like the wind. Those types of people typically have no idea where it is coming from or where it is going, but only that it is windy. In other words, people who take the literal, carnal interpretation of things cannot understand those who speak of spiritual things. Then Jesus pointed out the greatest contradiction or irony: a teacher like Nicodemus should know such things.[1] But in reality, how could Nicodemus come to such a conclusion. Nicodemus was a literalist, and Jesus taught by the Spirit.

One conclusion to draw from this is that Jesus used humor to teach, and although at times he used it to counter his opponents, he also used it positively to help his audiences see beyond their engrained assumptions. For Nicodemus, Jesus' sense of humor yielded a positive change in momentum as John 3:11, footnote b mentions.

Hyperbole

Defined as an intentionally exaggerated comparison or figure of speech, a hyperbole seeks to draw the reader in by calling attention to certain inconsistencies of mortal existence. Some authors are prone to hyperbole, and Jesus in particular, seems to have appreciated the effect this teaching method had on his audiences. On a number of occasions, Jesus used hyperbole to teach eternal truths. Many times the use of hyperbole appears directed at the disciples or interested listeners rather than those who confronted Jesus or challenged him.

Toward the end of his life, Jesus used a hyperbole that is sometimes overlooked or obscured through the process of translation. When Jesus was challenged during his final week of life, he responded publicly in a way that was more critical and condemning than perhaps any of his earlier speeches had been. Some refer to this section (Matthew 23) as Jesus' final condemnation of the Pharisees; and in that section, certain types of expression are preserved that are found nowhere else in the teachings of Jesus. One saying in particular stands out as a well-crafted hyperbole.

Jesus taught, "Ye blind guides, which strain at a gnat, and swallow a camel" (Matthew 23:24). The passage caught the attention of the Prophet Joseph Smith, perhaps because of the recognizable difficulty of the English wording of this verse. The Joseph Smith Translation offers an explanation of its meaning, although it leaves the difficult wording intact ("You blind guides, who strain at a gnat, and swallow a camel; who make yourselves appear unto men that ye would not commit the least sin, and yet ye yourselves transgress the whole law").[2] The meaning seems clear, but the odd wording creates a mental picture of a person trying to grab gnats out of the air with his teeth.

Instead, the Greek text of this passage should be translated, "You blind guides, who strain out a gnat, but swallow a camel" (author's translation). The custom in question, of using a cloth strainer to strain one's drinks for insects prior to consuming them, was practiced by Jews as part of their efforts to remain clean and kosher. Certainly Jesus did not mean that they literally swallowed camels, but the metaphor of swallowing a camel—the largest land animal in Judea and Galilee—conjures up the idea that they would swallow anything, or literally believe anything, except for the truth because they were so narrowly focused on doctrinal minutia.

Perhaps Jesus' most famous hyperbole came as part of his response to the rich young man who wanted to know which commandments he could emphasize to receive a greater reward for his actions. The rich young man expressed sentiments that were real and human: he wanted to know if certain commandments were greater than the others. His concern was that he was already obedient but he had not received the reward or the promise he had anticipated: "All these things [the commandments] have I kept from my youth up: what lack I yet?" (Matthew 19:20). Therefore, he wanted to know where he could redirect his spiritual energies. Perhaps it was simply an issue of focus, as his question seems to imply. Jesus then asked the rich young man to do something that would try his very soul. Jesus asked him to "sell that thou hast, and give to the poor, and thou shalt have treasure in heaven: and come and follow me" (Matthew 19:21). The story of the rich young man ends with him leaving sorrowfully. It does not indicate whether he did as Jesus had taught, but only that he was sorrowful because he had been asked to make such a great sacrifice to receive the reward he wanted.

At that point in the story, the Savior turns to his disciples to offer further understanding for what had just taken place. He taught them, "a rich man shall hardly enter into the kingdom of heaven. . . . It is easier for a camel to go through the eye of a needle, than for a rich man to enter into the kingdom of God" (Matthew 19:23–24). There have been many clever attempts to find in this saying an encoded message about a gate called the eye of the needle, or perhaps a certain textual confusion between the Greek words for camel and rope.[3] But owing to Jesus' teaching style and the disciples utter shock at what Jesus had said, it is certain that those who heard him say it thought he meant a real camel and a real sewing needle. The saying was intended to be dramatic, and it caused the disciples to ask the most important question, "Who then can be saved?" (Matthew 19:25).

This hyperbole drew the attention of his audience (the disciples) and helped them see something that they may have overlooked. Jesus taught them the most important truth when they were ready to hear: "With men this is impossible; but with God all things are possible," even getting a camel through a needle's eye (Matthew 19:26).

The pattern of using hyperbole to send a message can be seen in the following examples from Jesus' teaching. After teaching how thoughts are related to action in respect to adultery and fornication, Jesus taught,

"And if thy right eye offend thee, pluck it out, and cast it from thee: for it is profitable for thee that one of thy members should perish, and not that thy whole body should be cast into hell" (Matthew 5:29).[4] Again, in the same sermon Jesus taught his disciples, "And why beholdest the mote [splinter] that is in thy brother's eye, but considerest not the beam [log] that is in thine own eye? Or how wilt thou say to thy brother, Let me pull out the mote [splinter] out of thine eye; and, behold, a beam [log] is in thine own eye?" (Matthew 7:3–4). In teaching the disciples how to handle sacred things, the Savior taught, "Give not that which is holy unto the dogs, neither cast ye your pearls before swine, lest they trample them under their feet, and turn again and rend you" (Matthew 7:6). All of these examples attest to the importance of hyperbole in Jesus' teachings. It caught the attention of his listeners and drew them in to see greater spiritual meaning.

Dealing with Sarcasm from Family Members

Sarcasm is today frequently used but rarely appreciated; although it does not appear that Jesus directly used sarcasm in his teachings, on at least one occasion his family members derided him with words that now appear very sarcastic. The Gospel of John sets the stage for the confrontation between Jesus and his brothers by carefully pointing out two significant problems prior to entering into an account of the story. According to John 7:1–2, the opposition to Jesus had grown so significant in Jerusalem that he was no longer welcome in Judea (the KJV uses the word "Jewry") and that Jesus wanted to travel to Jerusalem (the heart of Judea) in order to participate in the Feast of Tabernacles. Jesus and his family were preparing to go to Jerusalem for the feast, but Jesus was in danger if he traveled there. John assumes, apparently, that audiences would understand that Jesus was devoutly religious and would want to attend, or perhaps even feel compelled, to travel to Jerusalem to keep the feast even though he could have observed it in Galilee.

Unfortunately, Jesus' family like many others faced its own share of internal disharmony and strife. According to John, Jesus' "brethren" did not believe him at that time (John 7:5). That word translated as "brethren" is the literal word for "brothers" and could also include "sisters" if they also were among those who did not believe. In Jesus' case, we learn in Matthew and Mark that Jesus was the oldest of at least seven children and that he had four brothers and at least two sisters (Matthew 13:55–56; Mark 6:3).[5] Therefore, Jesus likely faced some of the rivalries that are typical in large families, particularly those associated with families where the oldest child is extremely gifted.

While preparing to travel to Jerusalem, Jesus' brothers mocked him saying, "Depart hence, and go into Judaea, that thy disciples also may see the works that thou doest. For there is no man that doeth any thing in secret, and he himself seeketh to be known openly. If thou do these things, shew thyself to the world" (John 7:3–4). Although the Greek text does not preserve the tone that was used, they clearly show an underlying misunderstanding of Jesus and his mission. Moreover, they offer a distinct challenge for Jesus to prove who he was as well as a sarcastic appraisal of what Jesus meant to them. The Satanic temptation of offering Jesus a way to prove himself to the world had resurfaced through his brothers' taunt.

Fundamental to their approach is the assumption that Jesus' disciples in Galilee (the Twelve appear in the verses immediately preceding this story [John 6:67]) mean little or nothing and instead real disciples should be sought in Judea. Furthermore, their sarcastic challenge asked the simple question of whether Jesus' miracles and teachings were somehow meant to prove who he was. That idea could form part of the purpose of Jesus' miracles, assuming they meant that the miracles and teachings would lead Jesus' followers to believe in him as Savior and Messiah.

Perhaps the most profound lesson arising from this interchange comes not in how Jesus used humor in his response, which he did not do, but rather in how he dealt with cutting humor used against him. Rather than respond in kind, in this case sarcasm, Jesus neither backed off nor appeared intimidated by the challenge. Instead, he offered the following clarification of his mission and how it would eventually unfold. He taught them, "My time is not yet come: but your time is alway ready. The world cannot hate you; but me it hateth, because I testify of it, that the works thereof are evil. Go ye up unto this feast: I go not up yet unto this feast; for my time is not yet full come" (John 7:6–8). The meaning of verse 6 in particular is difficult. The Greek meaning can be appreciated in the following translation, "My right time is not here yet, but for you it is always the right time" (author's translation). Jesus seems to be offering a slight rebuke, suggesting that if he were to travel to Jerusalem for the wrong reasons, it would somehow become the wrong time for him (this situation is realized in John 7:32 when a crowd attempted to arrest him but could not because "his hour was not yet come" [John 7:30]).[6]

Jesus handled the criticism carefully, choosing words that do not betray an underlying seething conscience or a rattled sense of self. But Jesus privately wanted to attend the temple as the story implies. John records that Jesus' brothers left for Jerusalem to participate in the feast and that when they were gone, Jesus "went . . . also up unto the feast, not openly, but as it were in secret" (John 7:10). Jesus appears to be deeply religious in this story, but because of a sarcastic challenge he changed his plans to accommodate both his desire to be in Jerusalem and at the same time not succumb to the taunting of family members. Jesus provides a personal insight into how these feelings could build up and cause one to miss some of the blessings of temple attendance when he taught, "Therefore if thou bring thy gift to the altar, and there rememberest that thy brother hath ought against thee; Leave there thy gift before the altar, and go thy way; first be reconciled to thy brother, and then come and offer thy gift" (Matthew 5:23–24).

Interestingly, two chapters later in the Gospel of John, a man whom Jesus healed was rigorously challenged because of his newly found faith when he was questioned on how Jesus had healed him. The Pharisees were trying to determine whether the healing constituted an act of work and therefore a violation of the Sabbath laws. In the ensuing interrogation, the man's responses became sarcastic just like the brothers of Jesus: "I have told you already, and ye did not hear; wherefore would ye hear it again? will ye also be his disciples?" (John 9:27). The man's interrogators responded similarly, "Then they reviled him, and said, Thou art his disciple; but we are Moses' disciples" (John 9:28). The outcome in these stories is quite different, showing how strongly the use of sarcasm can shape the process of events. In the case of Jesus' brothers, they converted and later believed in Jesus (Acts 1:14; 1 Corinthians 15:7) whereas many of the Pharisees continued to oppose Jesus.[7]

SUMMARY

Jesus both used and experienced humor in his life. From Nicodemus' silly and humorous question to the biting sarcasm of unbelievers, Jesus responded by offering carefully worded explanations and sometimes by posing challenging questions that spoke beyond the scope of the original dialogue. At times, those who treated Jesus with sarcasm wanted him to become angry or to use sarcasm in return, but Jesus' refusal to stoop to that level sometimes resulted in conversion or softening of hearts.

Jesus also used humor in his teachings; he was particularly fond of hyperbole and dramatic metaphor. These attention getters drew audiences in; they captured the hearts and minds of disciples and interested onlookers alike. Hyperboles are scattered throughout Jesus' teachings and the Gospels consistently preserve this hallmark feature of the Savior's teachings. At times it may have been difficult for Jesus to respond in ways that did not come across as sarcastic or challenging because of his sharp wit and intelligence. One such story is recorded in Matthew 22:41–46 when Jesus challenged the Pharisees regarding how the Messiah could be both David's Lord and David's son. They could not answer the question, causing Matthew to note, "And no man was able to answer him a word, neither durst any man from that day forth ask him any more questions" (Matthew 22:46). But Jesus refrained from certain sarcastic conclusions that could arise from the interchange with the Pharisees. He used humor in positive ways to teach the gospel, and he experienced negative humor that challenged him regarding who he was and the purpose of his mission.

Fundamentally, it appears that Jesus' use of humor was intended to control the direction of certain discussions and to deflect certain criticisms. At times he used humor to evoke poignant questions; certainly Jesus' used humor intentionally. As the greatest teacher, Jesus was fond of certain types of humor, but it does not permeate all of his speeches. Instead, it is limited to a few instances where it advanced his doctrinal discussions.

ATTRIBUTE 10

Avoiding Confrontation
By Not Answering

JESUS' ANSWERS AT A GLANCE:

- Jesus is depicted at times as ignoring questions posed by certain individuals (Matthew 15:22–23), although continual pleading would induce him to respond
- Jesus rarely asked questions of his opponents, but he answered their questions even when their intent for asking was in question
- Jesus frequently answered challenging questions with questions
- When the disciples asked questions of Jesus, they received answers. Sometimes those answers were hard to understand (Matthew 20:20–29), but at other times his answers were easy to understand (Matthew 13:36–43)
- When answering questions, the Gospel authors do not record whether Jesus answered unwillingly, with sarcasm, out of exasperation, or any of the other verbs that often accompany answers given in volatile situations

HOW JESUS RESPONDED TO
QUESTIONS WITHOUT ANSWERING

One continual source of interest is the relationship that exists between

Jesus' mortal personality and his divine and exalted personality. In other words, can we learn what Jesus is like now through learning about him during his mortal ministry? The right answer could help us come to Jesus more fully. Without further prophetic direction on the issue, it may be that the question will remain unanswered. However, one of the most compelling reasons for studying Jesus' mortal life is the belief that in knowing him in mortality, we will know him better in eternity and be able to follow his will more closely. This book has specifically looked at Jesus' teaching style and what attributes contributed to making him a great teacher. But an underlying point of interest is that knowing the mortal Savior may indeed increase our understanding of the immortal Savior.

In the arena of New Testament studies, new texts are discovered on a fairly regular basis. Some of these texts are found in archeological digs and others are found in existing collections where the original catalogue information has been lost. Some manuscripts simply surface through the black market or through other shady sources. Nearly every time this occurs, a discussion takes place of whether the text accurately presents any valid historical information about Jesus or his words, or how the text compares to other early Christian writings. Detecting forgeries, whether ancient or modern, is difficult business. And generally scholars rely on the physical artifact—the manuscript—to answer such questions. But when the artifact itself is not old enough or interesting enough, there is often a push to argue that the text itself is older than the actual manuscript. For example, a book may be published quite recently, but the text it contains is very old. Sometimes this is made possible through an older reference to or a quotation of the text by a third party observer.

For example, the recent "discovery" of a fragment of the Gospel of Judas raised significant questions concerning the historical accuracy of its text and the New Testament accounts of Judas' betrayal of Jesus. This scene was repeated for both the Old and New Testaments in past generations with the discovery of the Nag Hammadi codices (1945), the Dead Sea Scrolls (1947), and the forgery known as the Secret Gospel of Mark.[1] The problem with the discovery of the Gospel of Judas is that the artifact could not be dated earlier than the fourth century AD, at least three hundred years after Jesus' death. Therefore, scholars must argue that while the artifact is late, the text it contains is considerably earlier.[2] But how can anyone know that a fourth century document preserves the actual words of Jesus, or any historical information about Jesus in the first century? One of the ways to do this is to determine if the text coincides with the known teachings and characteristics of Jesus of Nazareth; in other words, we ask ourselves whether it fits the known style of Jesus. In this chapter we will look at a characteristic of Jesus' teaching style that is unique to him; when we identify its presence, we are able to determine with some confidence that the saying does genuinely go back to Jesus.[3] Interestingly, this feature rarely ever appears in the forgeries that have been discovered in the modern era.

A UNIQUE CHARACTERISTIC OF JESUS' TEACHING STYLE

There are a few traits of Jesus' personality that stand out as unique to him and of which we are now aware; certainly others have been lost to history. Jesus had a distinct habit in mortality of offering answers that did not answer the specific question addressed to him even though the questions presented to him were quite clear and straightforward. In other words, sometimes Jesus would give answers that did not answer the question originally asked of him. Interestingly the Gospel authors also record that when Jesus answered in this way, his audiences seemed satisfied with the answer. Although not every example turned out this way, in several instances it appears that by offering an answer to another question, his audiences seemed to accept it without further comment.

To some this might appear to be deceptive or dodging an answer, but Jesus used it with great skill in his teaching; perhaps, it can also tell us something of his own immortal personality. It seems that in prayer we find that some questions we ask go unanswered but that the Lord provides answers to other questions that we have not asked. What would our lives be like if all of our prayers were answered in the ways that we wanted them to be. Rarely, if ever, can we engineer our own fate and destiny with the same accuracy and direction that the Savior can and does through not responding to all of our questions when we believe we need answers. In fact, the well-being of mankind would possibly be in jeopardy if all of our prayers were answered in the ways we wanted. We would not necessarily want our existence to be a cumulative result based solely on yes answers to all of our petitions. This habit of not answering certain questions extends back to Jesus in mortality.

Consider for a moment the question a small group of Pharisees and

Herodians extended to Jesus after he had entered Jerusalem for the last time. They came to him and asked, "Master, we know that thou art true, and teachest the way of God in truth, neither carest thou for any man: for thou regardest not the person of men. Tell us therefore, What thinkest thou? Is it lawful to give tribute [pay taxes] unto Caesar, or not?" (Matthew 22:16–17). The trap was so obvious that Matthew reports, "the Pharisees . . . took counsel how they might entangle him" (Matthew 22:15). Jesus also pointed out the obviousness of the trap: "Why tempt ye me, ye hypocrites?" (Matthew 22:18). Perhaps because they had asked the question in poor faith and with the intent to entangle Jesus in his words, he did not feel obligated to answer them in any way. But he did offer an answer, but it was not to the question that they asked.

Following the well-known story, Jesus asked that someone bring him a drachma (translated in the KJV as a "penny"). With the drachma in his hand, he asked those around him whose image was on the coin, to which they answered "Caesar's" (Matthew 22:21). Everyone knew whose image was on a drachma just as we know today whose image is on a penny. The question may have been insulting to the Pharisees because it implied that they needed such an obvious answer pointed out to them. To make the point even more obvious, Jesus then taught, "Render therefore unto Caesar the things which are Caesar's; and unto God the things that are God's" (Matthew 22:21).

The apparent simplicity of the answer disguises its inherent complexity. On the most basic level, Jesus taught that the coin bore Caesar's image and so it should be given to its rightful owner, but not necessarily because of an implied tax burden. But Caesar did not actually own the coin that was in Jesus' hand unless the Gospels have passed over a significant detail of the story. The coin actually belonged to someone in the audience, perhaps to one of the Pharisees who had asked the question. Another issue with the story is that Jesus did not actually answer the question, "Is it lawful to give tribute unto Caesar?" In other words, was it legal and appropriate to pay taxes? What Jesus actually answered was the question of what to do when someone finds a coin belonging to Caesar or belonging to God, but we cannot be certain whether he felt that Roman taxation was illegal as the question implied.

The underlying question is whether Jesus endorsed the practice of paying taxes to Rome. Some of his contemporaries had very strong opinions concerning paying taxes and believed that paying taxes represented a pro-Roman, and therefore, an anti-Jewish attitude. What his questioners wanted to know was whether Jesus would pay his annual taxes, or whether Jews should pay their taxes to Rome. Some even thought that Jews should rebel against Roman taxation and governorship. They wanted to know what Jesus thought about paying taxes, perhaps because they respected his opinion or they wanted to turn people against him as Matthew seems to indicate. Certainly, they could use his answer either way to demonstrate an anti-Jewish attitude if he endorsed the paying of taxes, and they could also claim that he was anti-Roman (a possible criminal offense) if he forbade the paying of taxes. At the end of the conversation, however, we only learn that if we find a coin belonging to Caesar we should give him what belongs to him, but we can only extrapolate whether that meant he was pro-taxation. His Pharisaic and Herodian interrogators certainly felt that the answer was ambiguous because they were unable to produce any accusation from Jesus' response; their trap obviously proved futile in this instance.

This first example shows that in certain situations, when those asking the questions had evil intentions, Jesus avoided answering their specific question. That may lead to the conclusion that this teaching method is applicable to situations where our audiences are hostile and challenging, but we will see below that the non-answers were used in a variety of different situations with different results. Human nature might lead us to believe that this is deceptive, but Jesus used it to great advantage and with particular skill, thus furthering his ability to teach the gospel.

ANOTHER NON-ANSWER: THE WOMAN TAKEN IN ADULTERY

Perhaps the most famous instance of a non-answer takes place when Jesus was asked to cast judgment on a woman who was caught in adultery. In the story, a group of Pharisees brought to Jesus a woman whom they had caught in the very act of adultery, making the legal question of the case quite straightforward. Apparently, the Jews who questioned him thought that Jesus would condemn the woman and recommend according to the law of Moses that she be stoned.

The charge against the woman—adultery—might actually hinge on a fairly rigid interpretation of one of Jesus' earlier sayings (explaining why there is no mention of her partner in adultery). Jesus had taught, "That whosoever shall put away his wife, saving for the cause of fornication, causeth her to commit adultery: and whosoever shall marry her that is divorced committeth adultery" (Matthew 5:32). Based on this teaching, the woman in question may actually have been a remarried divorcee, whom the Pharisees were now accusing of being an adulteress. Certainly this was a highly nuanced legal question.

Again, the question is intended to make Jesus seem to be either anti-Roman or anti-Jewish, depending on which answer he gave. When they put the question to Jesus, he "stooped down, and with his finger wrote on the ground" (John 8:6). Finally, after some pressure and continued asking, Jesus offered an answer. To the question of whether the woman should be stoned, Jesus said, "He that is without sin among you, let him first cast a stone at her" (John 8:7). Often discussions of this passage focus on the legal issues involved as well as Jesus' authority in this situation, but one rarely discussed aspect is how Jesus effectively answered their question without offering any answer at all. Based on what Jesus said, we cannot conclude whether he found the question silly, insulting, biased, petty, or difficult. We have no way to know how Jesus would have judged the case: we may infer an answer, but we do not have Jesus' answer to the original question.

Simply said, Jesus answered in a way that shifted the blame and focus away from the woman and onto her accusers, but it did not answer the question they had asked specifically. Jesus answered the question of whether one can stone someone if that person has sinned, but no one had asked that question. Jesus' diversionary answer diffused a volatile situation.

Again, we see that Jesus used this type of teaching method in a hostile situation and that he effectively managed the situation by not responding to a question. In this particular situation, the answer also permitted Jesus to show compassion to the woman in the story without the trouble of becoming embroiled in an all out war of words with his enemies.

Jesus' Declaration: "I and My Father Are One"

While at Jerusalem for the Feast of Dedication, Jesus went to the temple to worship, and while in the temple, a small group of Jews approached Jesus and asked him, "How long dost thou make us to doubt?

If thou be the Christ, tell us plainly" (John 10:24). Although Jesus had the opportunity to testify that he was the Messiah (the Christ), he instead responded in a way that did not specifically answer the question, which could have easily been answered with a simple, "I am" or even "I am not."

Instead, Jesus chose to speak of the sheep that the Father had given him. In testifying of his sheep, Jesus said, "I and my Father are one" (John 10:30). Unfortunately, the King James translation includes the word *my* in the translation, a word that is not in the Greek text.[4] According to the Greek text, Jesus actually said, "I and the Father are one" or "Father and I are one and the same" (author's translations). What he meant by this phrase is not entirely clear—he could have meant "I and the Father are one and the same being" or "I and the Father are one in purpose," or he possibly could have meant "I am the Father." The wording is sufficiently ambiguous to permit a variety of interpretations. That the Jews took him to mean something negative is clear from the Gospel of John.

After hearing Jesus utter this phrase, "the Jews took up stones again to stone him" (John 10:31). They thought he had committed blasphemy by claiming to be the Father or claiming to be God or saying something akin to that. What followed is perhaps Jesus' most carefully crafted non-answer in the entire New Testament. As they prepared to stone him (John noted somewhat sarcastically "again"), Jesus asked them a rhetorical question: "Many good works have I shewed you from my Father; for which of those works do ye stone me?" (John 10:32). This time his accusers saw Jesus' diversionary answer and pointed out that, "For a good work we stone thee not; but for blasphemy; and because that thou, being a man, makest thyself God" (John 10:33).

Their retort to Jesus' question was not entirely fair either because Jesus did not actually say that he was God, but they believed he implied it. Those who intended to stone him for such an implication certainly lacked definitive proof in this instance. The fact that the evidence is so slim is likely the reason that no one threw a stone, thus giving Jesus an opportunity to speak. Stoning Jesus for something he had implied would have certainly been hard-hearted; and this story in particular seems to imply that the attempted stoning may have resulted from an accumulation of grievances rather than frustration over this issue alone.

Because the Jewish audience was still fixated on the issue of blasphemy, he offered a diversionary question that again did not answer their original question. His answer this time was, "Is it not written in your law, I said, Ye are gods?" (John 10:34). This quotation comes from Psalm 82:6, where the Lord speaks to the premortal congregation of "gods." In Psalm 82, the premortal "gods" complain that the wicked rule on the earth and that unjust judges administer the law, to which God teaches them that they will have the chance to correct this wrong: "Ye shall die like men, and fall like one of the princes" (Psalm 82:7). The basic outline of the Psalm suggests that the premortal spirits ("gods") complained of the wickedness of humankind on the earth. To remedy the problem, those same premortal spirits would later come to earth and assure that the wicked did not reign and that judgment would be administered fairly.

From this Psalm, specifically verse 6, Jesus drew a logical conclusion: "If he called them gods, unto whom the word of God came, and the scripture cannot be broken; Say ye of him, whom the Father hath sanctified, and sent into the world, Thou blasphemest; because I said, I am the Son of God?" (John 10:35–36). In other words, if God called the premortal spirits "gods," and Jesus only claimed to be the "Son of God," (probably understood as "son of God" rather than "Son of God"), then technically Jesus' accusers were greater than he because they were gods and he was only God's son.

The answer is technically and formally brilliant but is built upon a number of assumptions that raise serious questions. First, Jesus says that the Psalms are "your law" and that they cannot be broken. In reality, Jews viewed the book of Psalms much as we do today; that is, they are wholesome poetic literature with hymn-like qualities. Some of the Psalms were sung in Jesus' day, but not many would agree with the statement that the book of Psalms was *the law*. They would reserve that designation for the five books of Moses (the Pentateuch). Not even the prophets would have been called "the law" as they used the term in the first century. They were all based on the law and taught the precepts of the law, but they were not the law itself. That is not to say that Jesus' statement is incorrect in any way; but in building his non-answer to their question, he inserted carefully worded concepts that would have caused his audience to reflect further on what he had said. It is as if he was building an answer with several different meanings.

A second issue arising out of Jesus' statement is that it did not really answer the question they had posed originally. They wanted to know whether Jesus was the Christ, but he taught them that they should not be angry with him because they had greater standing than he did. In a way, he used their self-congratulatory human nature to redirect their attention away from the issue at hand, while at the same time not answering them directly. The answer appears to have settled some of their concerns, but a number of them pursued the issue further, causing Jesus to find a way to escape their grasp (John 10:39). Jesus' words, however, sufficiently diffused a volatile situation that could have turned out differently. What is perhaps even more surprising in this story is the fact that Jesus never actually called himself the "Son of God" in this chapter. The title had been used in reference to Jesus on other occasions, but it is not part of this particular story (see John 1:34). So in formulating this particular answer, Jesus used a thought or teaching from another occasion, which appears to have passed by unnoticed.

In this instance, like the others preceding it, Jesus used a non-answer for those who challenged him, but unlike the preceding examples, Jesus appears to have attempted to divert their attention away from the original question only to be challenged again the same point. His second answer was again a carefully crafted non-answer that drew upon the language of scripture and the pride of those challenging him. This particular non-answer seems to be the most complicated of all of Jesus' non-answers.

HEALING BY THE POWER OF BEELZEBUB

According to the Gospel of Matthew, near the middle of Jesus' ministry, the opposition to Jesus became so great that he shifted to teaching publicly in parables while reserving his standard teaching style for his believers and disciples (Matthew 13:10–16). Shortly prior to this shift, Jesus' opponents tried to deal with the troubling question of how Jesus could heal others and perform the miracles that he did, which they apparently had witnessed frequently enough to testify that they were genuine occurrences. Certainly many have sought an answer to the disturbing question of faith healing when that healing occurs outside of one's own faith. It has never been easy to accept that others can be healed when they are of another faith, or when those being healed teach doctrines that we find unacceptable.

What is particularly troubling is when the person associated with the healing is someone we find offensive, unclean, or sinful. No doubt, Jesus' opponents thought of him as a sinner, as a blasphemer, and in many other negative ways. But even though they considered him to be all of those things, they had fairly clear evidence (some might even say indisputable) that he had healed certain individuals through the power of God. So they challenged him on the issue of healing by offering an interpretation of his miracles that has been offered in similar situations. They taught that Jesus did heal, but that he did it through the power of Satan.

Ironically, if they could know that Jesus performed miracles through the power of Satan, then certainly they could also seek such a clear testimony of whether they came from God. But likely their interpretation was intended to turn Jesus' followers against him and toward the Jewish ruling elite. It was probably aimed at undermining his popularity rather than being an accurate reflection on something he had said or done. According to the Gospel of Matthew, in response to their misguided interpretation Jesus said:

> Every kingdom divided against itself is brought to desolation; and every city or house divided against itself shall not stand: And if Satan cast out Satan, he is divided against himself; how shall then his kingdom stand? And if I by Beelzebub cast out devils, by whom do your children cast them out? therefore they shall be your judges. But if I cast out devils by the Spirit of God, then the kingdom of God is come unto you. Or else how can one enter into a strong man's house, and spoil his goods, except he first bind the strong man? and then he will spoil his house. He that is not with me is against me; and he that gathereth not with me scattereth abroad. (Matthew 12:25–30).

Jesus answered with a typical non-answer, this time presenting his antagonists with a serious doctrinal challenge to their assumption. Jesus stated, "Every kingdom divided against itself is brought to desolation" (Matthew 12:25).[5] At face value, the saying seems fairly easy to interpret. The logic is, Satan would not cast out his own kind (the demons) because that would result in the weakening of his own forces and, therefore, Satan would eventually fall. But was Jesus making a statement of policy regarding Satan's methods of deception or about Satan's eventual demise or something else entirely?

A few thoughts might help show the depth of Jesus' non-answer in this instance. First, is it true in all cases that Satan would not allow his own to be cast out in order to deceive? It seems in the overall scheme of things that Satan's focus is on winning the immediate battles that confront him while God's aim is to win the eternal war. So Satan continually scores small victories, but God will no doubt win the war. This would seem to support the idea that Satan would cast out his own because not doing so would imply foresight on his part, which is not typically one of his attributes. On the other hand, the variety of miracles throughout time, including the biblical accounts of false miracles, demonstrates that deceiving miracles do occur. Some famous examples of deceiving miracles are the priests of Pharaoh, who were able to copy some of Moses' miracles (Exodus 7–12) and the false prophet and sorcerer Bar-jesus (Acts 13:4–11). In fact Paul states, "Even him, whose coming is after the working of Satan with all power and signs and lying wonders" (2 Thessalonians 2:9). But perhaps the most dramatic miracle achieved through Satan's power will be a healing miracle that a false prophet of the latter days will perform on himself (a sure sign of false priesthood), the account of which John the Revelator recorded (Revelation 13:3). So the question really becomes whether Satan would cast out his own kind to deceive others. The answer seems to be an overwhelming yes!

At the same time, there is a question of the eventual downfall of Satan's work on this planet, which we know will occur once and for all at the end of the Millennium. The question then becomes whether Jesus is teaching that Satan's method—to deceive through casting out evil spirits—will eventually bring about his own downfall or whether Satan would limit himself to actions that would bring about his downfall sooner. Jesus' answer could be interpreted to mean that he was pointing out an internal inconsistency to Satan's method in opposition to God's plan of internal consistency and harmony. Indeed, Satan may do miracles to deceive, but eventually his focus on winning the immediate battles of life will result in losing the war entirely. Again, Jesus offered a brilliantly crafted, multivalent answer to the questioning of his opponents. Fortunately, or unfortunately depending on perspective, Jesus did not answer their direct question concerning whose power Jesus drew upon in the course of his miracles. Rather, he gave them an answer that pointed to the internal inconsistency of Satan. He could simply have answered that he healed by the power of God, but such an answer might have generated too much opposition prematurely.

This answer, unlike the others we've looked at, shows the depth of doctrine and the amount of substance in his non-answers. His non-answers were not simply distractions that were intended to divert his audiences away from the original question. This answer taught truth and great perspective, but it did not answer what they had originally asked.

It seems simple enough from our modern perspective to expect that a person would offer simple clarifications to perplexing issues when those questions were a result of years of misinterpretation or even popular misinterpretations of what Jesus had said. We expect our leaders to clarify ambiguities and issues when questions arise, but Jesus often did the opposite. Perhaps our own human perspective here stands in sharp contrast to divine perspective where a person may not appreciate the depth and clarity of an answer that is not given. Sometimes the greatest answer can be silence, or in the case of Jesus, the greatest answers were sometimes those that settled disputes rather than answering the antagonistic question asked by his opponents.

SUMMARY

One of the consistent features of Jesus' mortal personality and one of his greatest attributes as a teacher that is preserved in the Gospels is that he frequently offered answers that did not specifically answer the challenges of his questioners. Those non-answers were typically given to those who did not believe in Jesus or who wanted to discredit him.

So often our human situation is seemingly made more difficult by what we perceive to be unanswered questions or prayers. Some lose faith because answers to important questions do not come at what they perceive to be the right time. But often in retrospect we see that certain answers have been withheld for our own good and progress. We need an inspired architect to help us build our eternal existence, and that architect cannot rely on us to ask all of the right questions at the right times. At times it may be necessary to answer questions that have never been asked; at other times it is necessary to not answer questions that have been asked even when the inquirer seems desperate to know. In this respect, this teaching characteristic of Jesus overlaps with the divine attribute of not answering certain requests made in prayer even though the petitioner pleads for a response.

Jesus handled a number of volatile situations by using non-answers. He used this technique when his life was in danger. Sometimes, his responses held answers to many questions that were never asked. Perhaps that is the way he continues to speak to us even after the resurrection. In the Gospels we can detect that Jesus' most profound non-answers came when opponents challenged him, not from those instances when he was questioned by his believing disciples. To the faithful, his answers were always much more clear and precise, although even with the disciples he taught in parables that were not always clear to them (Matthew 13:36; John 16:17). Even they needed to look deeper into his teachings and ask questions to understand them.

As the exemplary master teacher, Jesus did not always respond to his sharpest critics, and he avoided answering some questions. This approach is certainly a characteristic of Jesus' teaching style and shows us today that there may be great value in using this method. Human nature yearns for explanations and information, but at times Jesus held back certain answers from those who were critical of him.

ATTRIBUTE 11

How Compassion Can Shape What We Say and Teach

EXAMPLES OF COMPASSION IN THE NEW TESTAMENT AT A GLANCE:

- On one occasion Jesus wept after seeing Lazarus' sister weep (John 11:35)
- When the disciples wished to send away a group of children, the Savior intervened on their behalf (Mark 10:14)
- Jesus healed a Gentile woman after she pled her case (Matthew 15:21–31)
- Jesus was willing to come into contact with those afflicted with leprosy even though he ran the risk of being infected
- Jesus sought for the release of his disciples on the night of the arrest (John 18:8)
- Jesus asked that the soldiers involved in crucifying him be forgiven because they did not fully understand what they were doing (Luke 23:34)

Perhaps one of the greatest attributes of the master teacher, and one that we can certainly emulate today, is the ability to feel charity or compassion for an audience. Jesus' peers, on several occasions, felt that he associated with undesirables, calling them sinners and publicans (Mark 2:15–16; Matthew 11:19). They did not see his actions as something worthy of a servant of the Lord nor conceive of the possibility that he may have associated with sinners and publicans because he loved them. Jesus had compassion on those who had been marginalized in society. Despite the challenges of his enemies, Jesus continued to minister to sinners and publicans. In chapter one, we saw that Jesus was a champion of the oppressed and advocated a ministry to the poor among the house of Israel. Without duplicating that discussion, we will look at stories in this chapter where compassion shaped the way that Jesus taught the gospel, where the love he felt may have determined what he taught.

We should note that the Gospel authors also saw in Jesus' character a certain firmness and strength, and that his compassionate actions were not viewed as a weakness but rather as a conscious attitude to care for and bless those who might otherwise miss hearing the gospel message.

Compassion is a tricky term. It can refer to someone who is always kind, considerate, and accepting, but it can also indicate a sign of inherent weakness and passiveness. Not all societies admire compassion. Some societies have seen compassion not as a virtue but rather as a weakness. In Jesus' day, compassion was not a virtue among those who favored Roman ideals and ways of thinking. Even among Jews, compassion does not appear to be something that should be cultivated and sought after. So in his first century context, the compassion of Jesus would have stood out to some as different and possibly even as a sign of inhered weakness. We expect him to be compassionate today, but the Gospel authors were careful to note that he was firm and compassionate. He could denounce the Pharisees for their sins and also weep at the death of a beloved friend. It is not clear what readers of the Gospels would have thought about the compassion of Jesus given their social upbringing, but to those who knew Jesus it would not be a surprise that he showed compassion for nearly all men and women.

THE STORY OF THE CANAANITE WOMAN

When we look at the ministry and message of Jesus, we think in terms of inclusiveness and acceptance of anyone who was willing to hear the gospel because in our modern world the idea that all who believe can be saved is readily accepted. Such a far-flung notion is certainly foreign to the New Testament and to the thinking of many Jews in Jesus' day. That is not to say that Jesus taught a gospel that was reserved for the house of Israel or for Jews only, but rather if he taught the salvation of the Gentiles, some of his countrymen would have considered that a strange notion. It may even have struck Joseph and Mary as odd when Simeon blessed the infant Jesus and said, "For mine eyes have seen thy salvation, Which thou hast prepared before the face of all people; A light to lighten the Gentiles, and the glory of thy people Israel. *And Joseph and his mother marvelled at those things which were spoken of him*" (Luke 2:30–33; emphasis added). It may be that Joseph and Mary marveled that Simeon had included the Gentiles in his description of the Savior's ministry. It is also possible that Jesus' disciples, men who were raised on the Jewish law, might have grown up with the perception that the Gentiles lived outside of the laws of God and were perhaps even un-redeemable.

With that worldview intact, Jesus traveled to the cities of Tyre and Sidon, which both lay outside the traditional borders of Israel. Those cities would have been inhabited by Hellenistic Greeks and Romans as well as a few Jews who had chosen to relocate there. There were Greek and Roman temples in those cities, and they celebrated Roman culture and ideas. That Jesus visited those Gentile cities is a surprise. Prior to visiting those cities, he had shown a strong penchant to stay in the smaller cities of northern Galilee and almost exclusively among his own countrymen.

His journey to Tyre and Sidon may have been one means of escaping the growing antagonism that was shown to him as well as a way of timing some of the last events in his life—the Mount of Transfiguration experience, the Triumphal Entry at Passover, and his death on the eve of Passover. We know that the journey to Tyre and Sidon took place during the months immediately preceding his death and perhaps those impending events weighed heavily on his mind. Unfortunately, these suggestions are only hinted at in the Gospels. But it is important to attempt to understand his mindset during those months prior because of how Matthew relates the story concerning the Canaanite woman.

According to Matthew, as Jesus entered into the regions of Tyre and Sidon, "a woman of Canaan came out of the same coasts, and cried unto him, saying, Have mercy on me, O Lord, thou Son of David; my daughter is grievously vexed with a devil. But he answered her not a word. And his disciples came and besought him, saying, Send her away; for she crieth after us" (Matthew 15:22–23). There are many reasons why the Savior did not answer the woman's pleas. As Matthew tells the story, her pleading became so distressing the disciples eventually asked Jesus to send the woman away, so we can be certain that he was aware of her request, but he chose to ignore it.

The momentum of the story shifts immediately after the disciples' request that the woman be sent away. Jesus responded to their appeal saying, "I am not sent but unto the lost sheep of the house of Israel" (Matthew 15:24). Whether the woman heard this response to the disciples or whether the disciples alone heard it is unclear, but at that point the woman, "came . . . and worshipped him, saying, Lord, help me" (Matthew 15:25). Now following the first response of the Savior, we would expect that the Lord would turn her away because she was a Canaanite and not one of the "lost sheep of the house of Israel." He had told his disciples that he was not sent to minister to those outside the covenant of Israel. But this woman had shown significant faith and when another Gentile showed such profound faith—the Centurion—Jesus extolled his great faith and healed his son (Matthew 8:5–13).

What happens in the story is not entirely unexpected given what the Lord had already said and given the attitudes that Jews felt toward Gentiles. What is surprising, though, is that the Lord rebuked someone who was seeking his help. In words that must have seemed abrupt and curt, the Lord said to the Canaanite woman, "It is not meet [appropriate] to take the children's bread, and to cast it to dogs" (Matthew 15:26). In other words the bread had been reserved for the children of Israel. We could look at this saying in many ways that would remove its apparent confrontational bent. Perhaps the saying represents a traditional Jewish view of Gentiles, perhaps the wording can be understood in different ways, and perhaps Jesus knew the woman would demonstrate greater faith after the rebuke and the disciples would see that Gentiles could have faith.

Whatever the reasons for giving such a strong rebuke, the story shows how the faith of an individual affected Jesus and apparently caused him to show compassion when it was not clear that he would do so. He had told the woman that it was not appropriate for him to give her the bread reserved for the children. She responded saying, "Truth, Lord: yet the dogs eat of the crumbs which fall from their masters' table" (Matthew 15:27). In other words, she was willing to take whatever scraps might fall from the table, a truly remarkable showing of faith and patience. At this point in the story, Jesus shows compassion to the non-Israelite and heals her daughter: "Then Jesus answered and said unto her, O woman, great is thy faith: be it unto thee even as thou wilt. And her daughter was made whole from that very hour" (Matthew 15:28). Her faith had made her daughter whole, but her faith also caused Jesus to change his stance from excluding her to blessing her. He was firm and compassionate.

Given the Lord's foreknowledge, it may be that he chose to use a rebuke because it both taught the disciples about preconceived notions regarding the faith of non-Israelites, and because the woman's faith grew as a result. And it provides a perfect example of compassion. Although this story involves several teaching styles—rebuke, challenge, healing—the concern that the woman shows for her daughter touches Jesus, who in turn shows compassion to her as a result.

THE HEALING OF LAZARUS

One of the most touching stories in all of the Gospels is the healing of Lazarus because it looks at Jesus' personal acquaintances and how he felt about his close friends and associates. What is fascinating is that there are no enemies or antagonists, no one is trying to trap Jesus with a question, and no one has demonstrated a lack of faith: it is simply a story of someone becoming sick and that someone was a close friend of the Lord's.

According to the Gospel of John, "Jesus loved Martha, and her sister, and Lazarus" (John 11:5) indicating that they were some of Jesus' closest friends.[1] John makes this note prior to telling the story, thus giving the impression that Jesus reacted in part because of that love. He told the disciples prior to traveling Bethany that Lazarus would not die, but that, "This sickness is not unto death, but for the glory of God, that the Son of God might be glorified thereby" (John 11:4).

In the meantime, after learning that Lazarus was ill, Jesus waited before traveling to see him in Bethany. During that wait, Lazarus died. When he had decided to travel to Bethany, he told the disciples, "Our friend Lazarus sleepeth; but I go, that I may awake him out of sleep" (John 11:11). John knew that the plan was always to heal Lazarus. The delay in traveling to see him was part of that plan so that the disciples could come to know the glory of God (John 11:15). So when Jesus arrived in Bethany and was greeted by Martha he had already planned to heal her brother even though she was not aware of that decision.

In their discussion concerning Lazarus, Martha expressed her faith in Jesus in several ways. She said to the Lord, "Yea, Lord: I believe that thou art the Christ, the Son of God, which should come into the world" (John 11:27), which is the most complete testimony borne of the Savior to that point in the Gospel of John. Although there may have been other equally strong testimonies that were being silently nurtured, Martha's testimony was the most profound. That testimony must have touched the Savior deeply as he prepared to do the very thing that she had implied he could do with the words, "I know that he shall rise again in the resurrection at the last day" (John 11:24). Jesus was about to show her that the raising of Lazarus would not have to wait until the day of resurrection.

Martha, having spoken with the Lord, sensed at some moment in the conversation that she should bring Mary, her sister, to the place where she had met Jesus. It is difficult to know what events in the past had transpired that had caused Jesus to feel such love for the family of Mary, Martha, and Lazarus, but John did note that Mary had performed a special act of service for him: "It was that Mary which anointed the Lord with ointment, and wiped his feet with her hair" (John 11:2). Because of that act, and probably many more reasons that are not mentioned, Jesus loved the sisters Martha and Mary. Martha had borne a powerful testimony of his calling and ministry and as Mary approached, the woman who had bathed his feet with her tears, Jesus was moved with compassion.

Interestingly, Mary did not need to speak to the Lord and bear testimony as her sister Martha had previously done. The change in momentum took place when Jesus saw her and the other friends of Lazarus weeping. That scene was enough to move him, so much so that he began to weep also. In the shortest verse in the New Testament, and in many ways the most profound, John describes the full depth of the compassion he felt toward his dear friends: "Jesus wept" (John 11:35). He had planned to heal Lazarus, he had told his disciples that they would travel to Bethany to heal him, but the faith of Martha and the scene of Mary weeping touched Jesus.

But raising Lazarus would cost Jesus dearly. There was a price to showing compassion. In the very next story in the Gospel of John, we learn that Caiaphas responded to the healing by convening a council to consider the matter. John records, "Then gathered the chief priests and the Pharisees a council, and said, What do we? for this man doeth many miracles. If we let him thus alone, all men will believe on him: and the Romans shall come and take away both our place and nation. And one of them, named Caiaphas, being the high priest that same year, said unto them, Ye know nothing at all, Nor consider that it is expedient for us, that one man should die for the people" (John 11:47–50). The plot to kill Jesus was thus hatched as a result of Jesus healing Lazarus.

In the next chapter the plot to kill Jesus was extended to include Lazarus, "But the chief priests consulted that they might put Lazarus also to death; Because that by reason of him many of the Jews went away, and believed on Jesus" (John 12:10–11). Truly Jesus showed great compassion to his friends, but that compassion ultimately threatened his life as well as the life of the person he had healed.

In the heated environment of the Gospels, amid conflict and challenge, and in a world where compassion was not highly sought after, we learn that Jesus' act of compassion came with a heavy price. John was not aware of whether Jesus knew the reaction he would receive, but Jesus acted out of love and accepted the consequences of his action.

It is not likely that we will have the need to perform the miracles that Jesus did during his mortal ministry. We can, however, still learn from his acts of compassion. Despite the costs and difficulties that would ensue as a result of raising Lazarus so near to the hotbed of contention—Jerusalem—Jesus showed love for his dear friends. He was not afraid to show his emotions and many reacted at seeing Jesus weep, considering it a genuine demonstration of love: "Then said the Jews, Behold how he loved him!" (John 11:36).

In our own teaching we might find a parallel to Jesus' actions as we seek to prepare ourselves in a way that will bless the lives of our students. There are many reasons to prepare for a lesson—fear, interest, concern, love, and even pride—but to prepare out of compassion, so that those whom we teach may grow and learn the gospel of the Lord, is one of the purest reasons to prepare ourselves.

SUMMARY

In a world where compassion was not highly touted or sought after, in a world where the strength of an individual was more important than humility, it is interesting to see that the Gospel authors preserved at least some evidences of Jesus' acts of compassion. They tell both sides of the

story, how Jesus was strong and powerful in situations where he was challenged, and they also tell stories where he showed great love and caring for
those who followed him. In those instances where love rather than conflict shaped what he taught, we see an extremely caring side of the Savior's
personality emerge. Perhaps the examples are limited because so much of
what he taught was dictated by the controversies that surrounded him.

After the resurrection, compassion seems to be a more dominant feature of the Lord's personality, and it continues that way today. Unfortunately the Gospels only mention it in a few instances, perhaps because of
the day and age in which they wrote and perhaps because of their audience. Compassion for many seems to be a nurtured attitude. It would be
fascinating to know whether it was an inherent or a cultivated attitude for
Jesus. The incompleteness of our sources, however, will not permit us to
know that fact.

Conclusion

A study of Jesus' personality and how we might apply his example to our own lives raises a number of methodological concerns. Some may feel that thinking of him in these specific ways overlooks the most important parts of his life—the Atonement and his Resurrection—and the emphasis on meaning that the Restoration has placed on those events. For people living after Jesus' death, he is now the Lord and God of salvation; these beliefs are the foundation of testimony. How we understand him now is difficult to disassociate with his identity when he lived on the earth. So, for example, because he is omniscient now would that imply that he was omniscient in his own lifetime, or because he is perfect now would that mean he was perfect to all laws of all dispensations or only to the law of his day and age (the law of Moses)? He is God, and the New Testament seems to tell the story of how he became God. Seeking to understand Jesus as a person who lived in the first century, particularly his mortal personality and characteristics is the closest that we can come to experiencing his life in mortality in our own day and age.

As we seek answers to the important questions about Jesus' life and how he lived it, we are confronted with the peculiar problem of differentiating the exalted, immortal Savior and the mortal Jesus. To further complicate this endeavor, we teach that whether we were to hear the voice of the Son or the voice of the Father, they would both declare unto us the very same thing. They would not contradict one another in any way or for any reason. Essentially we think of them as two separate beings who dwell in distinct and different tabernacles but who share the same will and purpose. To see one would be to see the other and to know one would be to know the other.

Even more difficult for us to comprehend is the fact that Jesus now enjoys the status of deity, but he also enjoyed that status prior to his birth (John 1:1). He was the God of the Old Testament, and he was the voice of the Lord to the prophets (Doctrine and Covenants 38:1–4). Given that he was God and is God now, is it possible for us to consider a moment in time between those two existences when he became God? And during that time when he lived on the earth, did he feel real human passions, was he tempted, and did he have a unique teaching style that we can learn from?

To fully plumb the depths of what the New Testament can teach us, let's consider exactly how revolutionary its message really is for us and how it provides insights to these questions. The New Testament authors, a collection of later followers of Jesus and eyewitness disciples, faced these very questions as they interacted with Jesus one-on-one or through the stories that they heard others tell of him. One of those authors—Mark—thought of him in human terms; he looked at him through human eyes and saw a man of passion and power. Unlike Mark, John thought of Jesus in terms of God coming to earth to save his people, or as deity who condescended to become our Savior. So the premortal Jesus was certainly a consideration for John as he presented the story. On the other hand, Matthew and Luke looked at environment, considered his birth, and early experiences, which shaped the way they told the story. They, like the author of the Gospel of Mark, looked carefully at the very human side of Jesus that they saw in their sources or that they saw in him when they knew him.

Mark, more than any other author, willingly considered Jesus as a person, a mortal whom people came to know. He wrote down people's impressions of him, that he seemed angry or disturbed, even if those impressions were wrong or raised troubling questions about Jesus' perfection. For Mark, the story of Jesus appears to be a story of how the humble Jesus of Nazareth fulfilled the will of the Father in all things and what people felt when they encountered him. He lived a remarkable, miraculous existence that drew followers from Galilee and Judea. From Mark's perspective we can learn how he responded to challenges, how he handled ridicule, and how he taught he gospel. We can make modifications in our own lives as we seek to be like Jesus. For Mark, Jesus set an example that could be followed.

Matthew and Luke wrote why Jesus was chosen and not someone else. Interestingly neither author pursued the reasoning that it was because of a premortal calling or identity, even though that was certainly part of the answer. Instead they pieced the story together through the Old Testament prophecies of him as well as the early experiences he had that reveal how revelation foretold of his special mission. The question of why Jesus instead of another person is answered in the birth stories, the genealogies, and eventually through his baptism and life. His life was foretold through prophecy and through his early experiences, he was anointed to be our Savior.

Matthew and Luke also left other important questions open, such as whom Jesus was prior to his birth, a question that John would seek to answer. For Matthew and Luke, Jesus was the perfect example that the prophets of old had foreseen. He then becomes part of the revelation of God's will and pattern for salvation, and therefore we should follow him to salvation. Following Jesus' example would be directly following God's will.

John, more than any other author, sought to understand how the premortal Jesus became the mortal Savior. Traits of the Savior in premortality are carried over into his mortal existence so that there is a direct link between those two states of existence. In the Gospel of John, Jesus "was made flesh, and dwelt among us," but he does not tell a birth story (John 1:14) because Jesus already had an existence prior to the one that John knew of. For John, Jesus is a primordial example of perfection and salvation, and he showed us the way to salvation. John, in some ways, emphasizes what Jesus said in mortality more than what he did, although he certainly placed his greatest emphasis on the final acts of the Atonement.

Each of these approaches to telling the life of the Savior has attracted millions of readers throughout time; and each of these approaches appears initially oriented at trying to record and preserve the story of earth's greatest teacher and inhabitant. They wanted to know who he was and how he did what he did. They sought to know him, and they documented their understanding of him in slightly nuanced ways. There was not a single, monolithic way to tell his story as they knew it or encountered it. This remains true even today, and even within the church of the first century some sought to emphasize certain parts of his life or to teach it from a different vantage point. Collapsing their voices into a single view has its benefits, but that approach cannot comprehend the nuances the Gospel authors sought to infuse into the story.

They sought to understand Jesus in their own ways, using the stories that they remembered of him to reconstruct his life in a way that substantiated what they had felt, seen, and knew to be true. Likewise, in seeking to understand who Jesus was and is, it is important to look into and seek the Jesus of history in order to feel what he did or see what they saw.

Of considerable importance for this study is also the definition of personality. Personality is a combination of environmental conditioning, inherited capacities and gifts, as well as learned attitudes and perceptions, thus comprehending the full spectrum of approaches of all four Gospel authors. Personality is something that we all develop over time and that may change through conversion, experience, personal growth, and other environmental factors. Jesus' personality, of which we know very little, manifests itself briefly in the gospel stories. But coming to understand how he maintained perfection in light of having inherited certain attitudes, capacities, and other attributes can also help us to comprehend and seek to redeem our own human experience. Our own personalities are part of our own human experience, and they provide us certain challenges and trials; and it is through our personality that we at times experience temptation.

Seeing Jesus' experience as parallel to our own existence also helps us seek perfection. Knowing that he faced genuine temptation can strengthen us through our own temptations. His own life can be a model for our own, or in his own words he taught, "I am the way, the truth, and the life: no man cometh unto the Father, but by me" (John 14:6). For this reason, and those mentioned above, seeking to know Jesus as he really was remains an important aspect of how we know him. That understanding has its origin in the first century and reveals how the men and women who knew him experienced the only perfect life ever lived.

In the end we have glimpsed the life of a wonderfully rich teacher, who taught using humor and wit, who frequently quoted scripture and at times used proverbs and parables. At other times he avoided answering questions and all the while he maintained a firm humble hold on his own status as a celebrity among his countrymen. He was and is an amazing teacher. This study has been an attempt to experience the richness that so many had the opportunity of experiencing in the first century. He changed many people's lives, more than any other single individual in the history of mankind. As we consider his life, we learn the life of a teacher with a profoundly simple message of hope. In his lifetime he had the occupation of a carpenter, but he was a teacher at heart and a Savior by calling.

The purpose of this book has been to see him for what he really was in mortality, in the months and years before the Atonement. In the gospel accounts, the message comes through with ringing clarity: Jesus was a master teacher of remarkable skill. He controlled defiant audiences and he taught truth to those who wished to follow him while at the same time he withheld certain truths from those who opposed him. Some of his teachings were delivered on multiple levels that could be understood in a variety of ways.

We sometimes think of Jesus as a carpenter and when asked about Jesus' occupation we often use that term to describe him. However, when we look at the way the disciples of Jesus described him, we learn that he was a teacher, healer, and Savior. Like Jesus, we are all teachers, whether that is through a formal calling or through the everyday experiences of life. We cannot say that there is a single approach to being a great teacher, although personality plays an important role in our ability to teach effectively. Perhaps we find it difficult to teach with proverbs or to avoid answering certain questions, but there are aspects of his teaching style that can help us improve our own teaching style. We can all use at least one or two of the characteristics of style that Jesus used. As we learn how he taught, we can perhaps improve in those areas where we share method and approach with the master. What is also very important is the process of beginning to see teaching as a deliberate skill that can be improved. Teaching is not simply something that happens to us when we need it to. But like Jesus we should develop our own style and use it consistently in certain situations. There are times for humor and times when silence is appropriate, and as we learn to model the master teacher we will both improve ourselves and share a moment with the greatest teacher of all.

Postscript

It is a surprising study to look back at how we as Latter-day Saints have thought about Jesus and his teachings. In doing the initial research for this book, I was quite surprised at how little we have focused on Jesus' teaching style, personal attributes, and personality. The content of his teachings—the doctrines—have received focused and careful attention, but for the most part those discussions are aimed at drawing out applications and only touch on their first century context briefly. Particularly sparse are studies that look at the methodologies Jesus employed, and how looking at his own methods of teaching we might improve our own teaching.

Our understanding of Jesus has grown exponentially as the clarity of the Restoration has cast its light on the texts of the New Testament. Looking back at the teachings of the Prophet Joseph Smith, it is obvious that the light of the Restoration enabled him to see the New Testament, Christian traditions, and even non-canonical writings (see Doctrine and Covenants 91) in entirely new ways. Passages such as John 1:18—"No man hath seen God at any time; the only begotten Son, which is in the bosom of the Father, he hath declared him"—made little or no sense after the First Vision. Of course someone can see God; Joseph knew that simple fact without a doubt, and so he realized in a powerful way that the Bible needed correction in some instances. Other passages may also have seemed incorrect after the Lord had taught his prophet more fully on a given subject. Paul's teaching, "There are also celestial bodies, and bodies terrestrial: but the glory of the celestial is one, and the glory of the terrestrial is another" (1 Corinthians 15:40), may have caused the Prophet to pause because he knew that there were actually bodies celestial, terrestrial, *and telestial*. Paul may very well have said only celestial and terrestrial for a variety of reasons, but the light of the Restoration made Paul's teachings now obviously incomplete.

Somewhere around the turn of the twentieth century, almost one hundred years after the light of the restoration of the gospel had illuminated Christian history, it became apparent that no one in the Church had yet written a comprehensive study of the life of Jesus. We cannot read the literature from that intervening period without recognizing how powerful the Restoration was for understanding who Jesus was. Profound statements were made about his ministry, his life, his death, and even regarding many things that were not included in the modern Bible. This period might rightly be called the revelatory beginnings of our understanding about who Jesus was and what he did. The period between Joseph Smith and the first LDS biography of Jesus can be characterized as interpreting Jesus' ministry in light of the Restoration. Our modern organization, practices, and approaches were discovered and discerned in the New Testament texts during this early revelatory period—the light of the Restoration even seems to encourage this in many instances.

But we still lacked a biography and other detailed studies; and owing to the simple fact that other major religions had produced many such works we, who could see Jesus more fully, lacked one. The initial efforts to produce a biography of Jesus received incredible attention; in fact, it received so much attention that its publication was endorsed, months before it appeared on bookshelves, directly by the First Presidency. The book in question—*Jesus the Christ*—was originally published in 1915 and according to the title page printed in our most recent editions, President Joseph F. Smith held the copyright. The copyright was renewed again in 1922 and 1949 by the presidents of the Church, and only in 1982 was the copyright passed over to Deseret Book Company.

No other study about the life of Jesus will likely have the impact that Elder Talmage's book has had for a number of reasons. First, Elder Talmage was given the council room in the Salt Lake Temple to write in, where he began his work in earnest on September 14, 1914, thus providing the author with a uniquely inspired setting. Second, as he completed the chapters, they were read to the First Presidency and assembled members of the Quorum of Twelve Apostles for acceptance, thus giving this book a unique endorsement that few, if any, books will ever enjoy. And finally, when the book was printed, the First Presidency made the following statement about it in the *Deseret Evening News* of August 14, 1915: "We desire that the work, *Jesus the Christ,* be read and studied by the Latter-day Saints, in their families and in the organizations that are devoted wholly or in part to theological study. We recommend it especially for use in our Church schools, as also for the advanced theological classes in Sunday schools and priesthood quorums, for the instruction of our missionaries, and for general reading."[1]

By the fall of 1915, the Church finally had an authoritative biography on the life of Jesus, one that was endorsed by Church leaders and that the Saints were directed to use in their Sunday schools, homes, and classrooms. It must have been an exciting time to finally read for the first time ever a comprehensive treatment of Jesus the Christ in light of the Restoration. The book was so successful, in fact, that a second printing was already being considered a month after the book was offered for sale.

For nearly fifty years, the book enjoyed an exclusive position on Latter-day Saint bookshelves; but in the 1960s, beginning with Bruce R. McConkie's publication *Doctrinal New Testament Commentary* (1965) and then later *The Promised Messiah: The First Coming of Christ* (1978), the four volume series *The Mortal Messiah* (1979–81) and eventually *The Millennial Messiah: The Second Coming of the Son of Man* (1982), members of the Church had a significant body of new literature on the subject of Jesus' life. Between Elder Talmage's publication and the 1960s, there were few publications that significantly altered the direction and scope of *Jesus the Christ*. In the 1950s Elder J. Reuben Clarke Jr. again began asking profound new questions about the Bible and its account of Jesus, questions that may have in fact influenced a younger contemporary—Bruce R. McConkie. Although many of Elder Clark's works were significantly influential in their day, only a few of his writings have received continued attention the way Elder Talmage's and Elder McConkie's have.

Before he was called to be an apostle, Bruce R. McConkie was faced with some interesting questions, some of which would induce him on a career of rewriting almost everything Church members had at their disposal on the life of Jesus. The challenges were these: Elder Talmage's work did not make any significant use of the Joseph Smith Translation of the Bible; it did not discuss the establishment of the Church in Jesus' day in any significant way, and therefore it was not clear what organization and structure the Restoration restored; and it did not significantly ask questions of the Bible's accuracy. There may have been other questions, but these seem to me to be the more obvious Bruce R. McConkie was asking in those early publications.

Elder McConkie's work has been characterized in a number of ways, and some of the early reviews of his work written by those outside the Church were considerably unfavorable. His detractors felt that he should have incorporated biblical scholarship to a greater extent, and like his predecessor Elder Talmage, he should have relied on recent scholarship rather than on some of the then outdated works such as those by Adam Clark, Frederic W. Farrar, J. R. Dummolow, J. Cunningham Geike, Alfred Edersheim, and others. But this criticism fails to appreciate what he was trying to do and the tradition he stood in. If Elder Talmage's work can be considered a Latter-day Saint interpretation of the life of Jesus, then Elder McConkie's was even more so. He carried the work of Elder Talmage forward rather than redirecting it. This careful methodological approach yielded impressive results and members have continued to flock to his publications because of what they represent and how they place Jesus in light of the Restoration.

WHERE WE ARE TODAY

We are now thirty years or more removed from these influential publications and contemporary scholars have again begun asking serious questions about Jesus and what he was really like when he lived his life in the first century AD. Many of the conclusions being advocated are contrary to faith. For example, some contemporary scholars see him as a cynical philosopher or itinerant charismatic teacher (rather than as a Savior of mankind), while others, who are less radical in their conclusions, see him as a miracle worker or rabbi-like teacher. More recently, many have questioned his divinity and dismissed him as a crank, crackpot, or promoter of a secret society.

At the turn of the twentieth century, an influential thinker named Albert Schweitzer began writing about the New Testament and asking questions in ways that continue to shape the way we carry out biblical research today. Shortly after completing his Ph.D., and at the young age of thirty-one he published a book entitled *The Quest of the Historical Jesus*. Before that volume appeared in print, he had given up his promising career as a biblical scholar and devoted his life to serving the poor and downtrodden in Africa. Many of his subsequent writings, which still focused on biblical interpretation and understanding, were written while he served in humanitarian efforts for the underprivileged. In his monumental work—*The Quest of the Historical Jesus*—he concluded that every generation of scholars and churchmen have made Jesus a part of their own modern world and into a reflection of themselves. In other words, our preconceptions about who he was have influenced our interpretations of Jesus so much that we are not able to determine who he really was and what he really did. Schweitzer labored under the opinion that the real, historical Jesus could be discovered only if the successive layers of tradition were peeled away so that one could have a clean glimpse of Jesus as he was in the first century.

One of the logical conclusions to Schweitzer's critique of the academy in the modern era has been for scholars to develop new methodologies to unravel the now convoluted picture of Jesus and find the "true" or "historical" Jesus, which should be differentiated from the Jesus of faith or from the Jesus of the church. Many scholars have devoted their lives to describing how the early church acted as a filter of the sayings and stories of Jesus; and, therefore, they seek to peel back these layers of tradition in order to see whom he really was. Perhaps some of this work is even a confirmation that the apostasy had a significant effect on the text of our bible (see Article of Faith 8).

In the era after Schweitzer, scholarship on Jesus' life has tended to focus on two descriptions of Jesus, that of the living historical person and what he has come to mean to his followers. Interestingly, Latter-day Saint scholars often drew upon the works of those scholars who were either reacting to the post-Schweitzer frenzy to find Jesus, or who were involved in the very quest to identify the historical Jesus. Early Latter-day Saint scholars, therefore, were often inadvertently making use of the arguments and historical data derived for those ongoing scholarly debates, but for very different purposes and objectives. This effort to draw from scholarship to enlighten our own Restoration perspective of Jesus continues today, and the quest that Schweitzer largely initiated still shapes the way scholars discuss the subject.

It is now time to look again at the sources that record Jesus' life and see how far we have come in understanding him. As Latter-Day Saints, we are not surprised to find that the story of Jesus has suffered over the

161

centuries from corruption and loss of text. Another startling shift is taking place as scholars are increasingly becoming polarized between what some have called conservative and liberal scholarship. Advances in understanding who Jesus was have been made by both parties, and for this reason and many others, it is time to reconsider Jesus again. That is not to say that this current study presents a new biography of Jesus, but rather a new look at one aspect of his life—how he taught the gospel—and how we can find new meaning from looking at his life again.

We have had the privilege of understanding Jesus in light of the Restoration, but that viewpoint, which is shared by a few in our day and likely only a handful of followers in his day, is only one means of understanding him. The vast majority of those who knew him when he lived thought different things about him: some hated him, some were indifferent, some felt he was too demanding, and some were intrigued by him. Only a few really committed themselves to following him. The many different vantage points on Jesus' teachings from the first century are reflected in the different viewpoints shared by billions of Christians today. The majority of Christians have not had the privilege of the Restoration to make sense of what he said and did. Some of those who listened to Jesus teach did not even have the privilege of the Spirit (John 7:39) to make sense of what he taught and said, while others knew of him and his teachings but did not respond to the call of discipleship.

In the process of learning about Jesus and his atoning sacrifice, I remember the very moment when my mind was flooded with the absolute knowledge that a man named Jesus lived in Jerusalem at the turn of the modern era and that for whatever reasons he was crucified between two criminals around AD 30. I had known about Jesus through faith, but knowing him as a living breathing person was something new, something rewarding. I cannot even today describe the impact that moment has had on me.

As these many different roads began to converge in the last few years, it became apparent to me that we needed to reconsider the history of Jesus again. The sources of information about Jesus' life—the apostles who wrote and Paul—provide rich, in-depth accounts of Jesus that offer many vantage points on who Jesus was. They did not seek to provide abstract biographies, but rather they found meaning in the way he handled certain volatile situations, in his miracles, in his heroic and tragic death, and in the way he taught the gospel.

There is no reason to correct the works that have previously been written on the subject; they have carefully described what Jesus' life and teachings mean, particularly for us in our day. Rather we should reenter the discussion and expand or build upon the foundation that has already been established. The Restoration has told us what Jesus meant, or perhaps should have meant to the many people who knew him or heard him speak, but who was Jesus to those who remained uncommitted or unsure? Was he more like Joseph Smith or Brigham Young or someone else? Was he hundreds of feet tall as some Christians thought or invisible as other Christians taught? What made so many people follow him, particularly after his death? Following his death, and perhaps even before it, there was not a single understanding of Jesus of Nazareth. Instead people were divided about what his life and death meant. The Restoration has interpreted the meaning of his life and death, but it can also offer several compelling insights into the person Jesus and how people perceived him. By bringing the light of the Restoration to shine on the story again, and considering the many valuable works that have preceded this one, we will see a powerful teacher at the very foundation and core of who Jesus was and is.

Notes

ATTRIBUTE 1

1. William R. Herzog II, *Prophet and Teacher* (Louisville, Kentucky: Westminster–John Knox Press, 2005), 50–57.
2. Richard Neitzel Holzapfel, Eric D. Huntsman, and Thomas A. Wayment, *Jesus Christ and the World of the New Testament* (Salt Lake City: Deseret Book, 2006), 28–41.
3. Brian J. Capper, "Essene Community Houses and Jesus' Early Community," *Jesus and Archaeology*, ed. James H. Charlesworth (Grand Rapids, Michigan: Wm. B. Eerdmans Publishing Co., 2006), 472–502.
4. Herzog, *Prophet and Teacher*, 121.
5. Herzog, *Prophet and Teacher*, 123–24.
6. Jennifer C. Lane, "Hostility Toward Jesus: Prelude to the Passion," *Celebrating Easter*, ed. Thomas A. Wayment and Keith J. Wilson (Provo, Utah: Religious Studies Center, Brigham Young University, 2007), 137–55.
7. Charlton T. Lewis, *An Elementary Latin Dictionary* (Oxford: Oxford University Press, 1992), 452.
8. Jesus denounced derogatory words in particular, like calling someone "Raca" or empty-headed (Matthew 5:22). On occasion, however, he did teach things that caused some of his followers to depart because those followers found some of his teachings offensive (John 6:60–66).

ATTRIBUTE 2

1. No New Testament texts preserve the word "rope" in place of "camel" suggesting that this is a modern confusion rather than an ancient one. See Holzapfel, *Jesus Christ and the World of the New Testament*, 92.
2. The word translated as "eagles" (*aetoi*) in the New Testament can also mean vultures.

3. The saying also contains an echo of Isaiah 49:24 and may be in part a commentary on the Isaiah passage.
4. Compare Josephus, *War* 2.8.1.
5. Holzapfel, *Jesus Christ and the World of the New Testament*, 79.
6. In John 7:3, 5 the KJV translates the word brothers (*adelphoi*) as brethren. Instead, the word literally refers to Jesus' siblings rather than the brethren of the church, a usage that is foreign to the New Testament.
7. M. L. Klein, *The Fragment-Targums of the Pentateuch I* (Rome, 1980), 61 quoted in Geza Vermes, *The Authentic Gospel of Jesus* (London: Penguin Books, 2004), 83.

Attribute 3

1. The attempts to stone Jesus resulted in nothing more than a threat to do him bodily harm. No actual stones were thrown, and if later rabbinic tradition is correct, an actual stoning was carried out by pushing a person off a cliff and then one of the witnesses to the stoning was directed to drop a large stone on top of the person. If the person was still alive at that point, the entire crowd was directed to then pelt the person with stones. In the Gospels, the threat of stoning appears more as a form of harassment than an actual attempt to throw Jesus off a cliff (for an exception see Luke 4:16–30). See M.-É. Boismard, "Stephen," in *The Anchor Bible Dictionary*, ed. David Noel Freedman, 6 vols. (New York: Doubleday, 1992), 6:209.
2. Holzapfel, *Jesus Christ and the World of the New Testament*, 51.
3. See Hebrews 5:9 for one of the earliest statements regarding Jesus' perfection. The doctrine of sinlessness is presented most clearly in the Book of Mormon. See Alma 34:8–16.
4. Milton C. Moreland, "Archaeology in New Testament Courses," *Between Text and Artifact*, ed. Milton C. Moreland (Atlanta: Society of Biblical Literature, 2003), 133–50.

Attribute 4

1. Interestingly the phrase "without a cause" in Matthew 5:22 is not found in the most ancient manuscripts of the New Testament or in the Joseph Smith Translation of the bible.
2. Although it is not absolutely clear that Jesus followed all of the kosher food requirements, his chief apostle did while he was with Jesus; and therefore, we might assume that Jesus kept kosher also.
3. It was not until the time of John Chrysostom (b. AD 385) that Christians were finally commanded to stop attending synagogue services and participating in Jewish festivals.
4. I am indebted to Amy-Jill Levine for this thought. She said, "Jesus does not have to be unique in all cases in order to be profound" ("How the Church Divorces Jesus from Judaism: Misusing Jesus," *Christian Century* [December 2006], 21).

Attribute 5

1. The verb translated as "astonished" (ekplêssô) has both a positive and negative connotation. See Frederick W. Danker and Walter Bauer, *A Greek-English Lexicon of the New Testament and other Early Christian Writings*, 3rd ed. (Chicago: University of Chicago Press, 2000), sv "ekplêssô."
2. The title Christ is a Greek translation of the Hebrew title Messiah. Both mean "anointed" and were not used as a part of a proper name for Jesus. Instead, in his lifetime some would have thought of him as "Jesus *the* Christ," but the name Jesus Christ is a later development when the title was widely accepted and recognized as referring to Jesus of Nazareth who was and is the Messiah.
3. For the specific references to the stories of Moses, see Bible Dictionary, sv "Quotations."

Attribute 6

1. Jonathan Reed, *Archaeology and the Galilean Jesus* (Harrisburg, Pennsylvania: Trinity Press International, 2002), 80–82.
2. During the temptations, Jesus quoted portions of Deuteronomy 6 and 8 in response to Satan's challenges, thus suggesting that he was intimately familiar with that text. See Matthew 4:4 (quotes Deuteronomy 8:3), Matthew 4:7 (quotes Deuteronomy 6:16), and Matthew 4:10 (quotes Deuteronomy 6:13).
3. The Greek translation of the Old Testament (the LXX) uses *theos* instead of El and thus reveals Jesus' reliance upon the Hebrew or Aramaic translation of Psalm 22 rather than the Greek.

Attribute 7

1. John 9:22 indicates that anyone actually claiming that Jesus was the Christ would be excommunicated from synagogue services, emphasizing their belief that he was to be thought of as Jesus of Nazareth or at least in more ordinary terms. The statement does not preclude following or listening to Jesus, but rather claiming that Jesus was anything more than a man from Nazareth.
2. In the apocryphal text of the Wisdom of Solomon, the author laments, "He professes to have knowledge of God, and calls himself a child of the Lord" (Wisdom 2:13 NRSV). Further, the author notes, "He calls the last end of the righteous happy, and boasts that God is his father" (Wisdom 2:16 NRSV).

   Jesus ben-Sirach, who lived in the second century BC, also spoke of a special relationship with deity that he described using the language of sonship. He spoke of God using this language, "O Lord, Father and Master of my Life" (Sirach 23:1).
3. The King James Version of the Bible capitalizes "Son" in the title but not the word "man." Some editions of the Joseph Smith Translation of the Bible do capitalize the entire title, but the Prophet Joseph Smith did not capitalize the title when the work of the New Translation of the scriptures was being carried out. The conven-

tion of capitalizing the title is modern. In the ancient manuscripts of the New Testament, the title is abbreviated, a way that early scribes showed respect for certain words, which may indicate that they would have preferred to capitalize it in all instances.

ATTRIBUTE 8

1. Danker, *Greek-English Lexicon of the New Testament and Other Early Christian Writings*, sv "peirazô."
2. Danker, *Greek-English Lexicon of the New Testament and Other Early Christian Writings*, sv "orgê."
3. Howard W. Hunter, "The Temptations of Christ," *Ensign*, Nov. 1976, 19–20; emphasis added.

ATTRIBUTE 9

1. Nicodemus used a common term of respect for Jesus (rabbi), which can be interpreted as "teacher" or "leader" but should not be interpreted in its modern sense as a trained rabbinic teacher or a leader among the Pharisees. The Gospel of John records that Jesus also referred to Nicodemus as a teacher, but instead John records the Greek word (*didaskalos*), thus avoiding the implications of Jesus hinting at the fact that Nicodemus had been leading people astray as a rabbi.
2. Footnote 24a for Matthew 23:24 contains slightly different wording for this particular JST passage. For the source of that different wording, see Thomas A. Wayment, *The Complete Joseph Smith Translation of the New Testament: A Side-by-Side Comparison with the King James Version* (Salt Lake City: Deseret Book, 2005), 64.
3. Holzapfel, *Jesus Christ and the World of the New Testament*, 92.
4. The Joseph Smith Translation labels this hyperbole a parable and clarifies that the saying should not be taken literally. See Matthew 5:20, footnote a.
5. The New Testament texts do not specify that Jesus' siblings were younger, but the implications of the virgin birth are that they were younger. Later traditions assert that they were Jesus' siblings from Joseph's first marriage, but those traditions are late and untrustworthy. The earliest tradition to interpret Jesus' brothers as his older stepbrothers is the 2nd century apocryphal text Protoevangelium of James 4.9.
6. The same word that is translated as "time" in John 7:6 is repeated in John 7:30 and is there translated as "hour."
7. There is evidence that some Pharisees believed in Jesus (Acts 15:5). Those Pharisees cannot, however, be connected with the interrogators of John 9.

ATTRIBUTE 10

1. For the most recent discussion of this possible forgery, see Stephen C. Carlson, *Gospel Hoax: Morton Smith's Invention of Secret Mark* (Waco, Texas: Baylor University Press, 2005).

2. For more information on this issue, see Thomas A. Wayment, "The 'Unhistorical' Gospel of Judas," *BYU Studies*, Nov. 2006, 45:21–25.

3. Interestingly, many scholars dismiss certain stories from the Gospels because they were not contained in the oldest manuscripts of the bible. For example, the story of the woman taken in adultery is not contained in many of the earliest manuscripts of the New Testament. (See Thomas A. Wayment, "The Woman Taken in Adultery and the History of the New Testament Canon," in *The Life and Teachings of Jesus Christ: From the Transfiguration through the Triumphal Entry*, ed. Richard N. Holzapfel and Thomas A. Wayment, 2 vols. (Salt Lake City: Deseret Book, 2006), 2:383–88.

4. The word "my" is included in italics in the KJV, thus indicating that the translators supplied the word and that it was not in the Greek texts they were using. "My," which could be expressed using a genitive construction, is not found in any Greek manuscript.

5. The accusation that Jesus healed by beelzebub is certainly a sarcastic challenge. Beelzebub means "lord of the flies" or the "fly god."

Attribute 11

1. The only other persons for whom that phrase is used is the disciple whom Jesus loved and another unnamed disciple. (For example, John 21:20 and Mark 10:21. See also John 15:9).

Postscript

1. James E. Talmage, *Jesus the Christ* (Salt Lake City: Deseret Book, 1982), xiii.

About the Author

Thomas A. Wayment is an associate professor of Ancient Scripture at BYU. He received a PhD in New Testament Studies at Claremont Graduate University. His research interests have centered on the life of Jesus and the formation of the early Christian church.

With Richard Holzapfel, he compiled and edited the three-volume work entitled *The Life and Teachings of Jesus Christ*. He is also the editor of *The Complete Joseph Smith Translation of the New Testament: A Side-by-Side Comparison with the King James Version*.

He and his wife, Brandi, are the parents of two children.